Crossi.

"Thompson proposes possible ways forward for the conversation between a traditional Lutheran theology of the cross and feminist approaches to the cross and suffering while offering a helpful synopsis and critical evaluation of each. This book will be helpful for theologians who value the cross as the central act of Jesus and also seek to understand feminist critiques or modifications of this symbol. Likewise, feminist theologians are reminded that Martin Luther's reforming approach to theology and his insistence that God is known deeply in human struggles make him a resource for today's personal, social and ecclesial struggles."

Marit Trelstad
Pacific Lutheran University, Tacoma, Washington

Crossing the Divide

Luther, Feminism, and the Cross

Deanna A. Thompson

FORTRESS PRESS

MINNEAPOLIS

CROSSING THE DIVIDE
Luther, Feminism, and the Cross

Cover image: © Photodisc
Cover and book design: Ann Delgehausen

ISBN: 0-8006-3638-4

Manufactured in the U.S.A.
08   07   06   05   04   1   2   3   4   5   6   7   8   9   10

Contents

for Linnea and Annika

Acknowledgments

The practice of theology depends upon conversations, worship, prayer, and connections with communities attempting to live out their theologies. I am indebted to many, many communities and persons, and I wish to thank them here: first, the church community in which I was raised, Prince of Peace Lutheran Church in Burnsville, Minnesota, especially Handt Hanson and Hal Weldin, who shaped my theological sensibilities and set me on my journey. I am grateful to St. Olaf College, the Paracollege, and especially Jim Farrell, who awakened me to feminism and the world beyond my limited white middle-class Midwestern vision; to Lutheran Volunteer Corps and Augustana Lutheran Church in Baltimore, Maryland—especially to Laurie Hoefer, who modeled exuberant feminist living and to Lola Willis, who taught me more about living the gospel than anyone I know; to Serene Jones and George Lindbeck at Yale Divinity School; and to the Graduate Department of Religion at Vanderbilt University, especially Sallie McFague, Peter Hodgson, Jack Forstman, and Gene TeSelle, all of whom shaped my development as a Lutheran feminist theologian. I thank Wendy Boring, Lillian Daniel, Verity Jones, and Kristen Looney for their enduring friendship and passion for theology rooted in ministry and for their powerful examples of motherhood; I also thank Hamline University, especially Tim Polk for his mentorship, friendship, theological wisdom, and zany sanity, and Earl Schwartz for his Jewish wisdom and his ability to read Christianity better than most Christians. I am grateful to the participants in the Upper Midwest Region Lilly Teaching Workshop, who helped me grow in my vocation as a teaching theologian; to First Fruits, a theological discussion group in the Twin Cities, where theology, teaching, and life always meshed in delightful ways; to the Workgroup in Constructive Theology, especially the members of the Christology subgroup, for their investment in life-and-death theology and their nurturing of my own thinking; and to Immanuel Lutheran Church in St. Paul, Minnesota, especially to Joy Bussert, for coffee conversations about what it means to be both feminist and Lutheran. I am also indebted to Michael West at Fortress Press for his theological insight and enthusiastic support of the project; to my student, Sean Silver, who ably aided me on the index; and to the readers of this manuscript. Thanks to Hamline colleagues Alan Silva and Alzada Tipton for their literary prowess and astute theological comments; Richard Pemberton for his probing theological questions and editorial expertise, Leonard Hummel for his Lutheran insight; Dianne Oliver—fellow traveler through the Ph.D. program, dear friend, and valued conversation partner—for her assistance with the feminist sections in particular; and my parents, Jackie and Merv Thompson, for their constant love, support, child care, and pastoral intuition with the manuscript. I also thank my extended family, especially my parents-in-law, Erna and Glenn Peterson, for their love, support, child care, and encouragement of this project. Finally, I owe an enormous debt of gratitude to my family: to my daughters, Linnea and Annika Thompson Peterson, to whom this book is dedicated, for the gifts of sheer grace that they are, and for their encouragement of "mama's book," and most importantly to my husband, Neal Peterson, for his unwavering love, constant support, and incredible patience, without which this book could not have been written.

Introduction

The cross alone is our theology.
—Martin Luther

No one was saved by the execution of Jesus.
—Rebecca Parker

Participants in Christian community cannot avoid the bloodied body of Jesus hanging from a cross. But what significance does this cross event have for Christians today? Contemporary theology plays host to a chorus of voices calling for an accounting of the church's long and active history of using the cross of Christ to inflict suffering upon the innocent. From blaming the Jews for Jesus's death, to the Crusades, to invoking the cross as justification for the silent suffering of women, Christianity must confront the ways in which its theology and resulting practices glorify and even cause undeserved suffering.

Among the alleged perpetrators littering the historical Christian landscape, few loom as large as the reformers of sixteenth-century Europe, those fathers of Protestantism obsessed with God's harsh wrath and judgment on deservedly damned human beings. Indeed, we need not wade far into the writings of reformer Martin Luther before we become submerged in what author Kathleen Norris calls the "scary vocabulary" of Christian speech. When heard with twenty-first-century ears, much of what Luther says and how he says it offends modern sensibilities: that the sinner must be *slain* by the cross of Christ, that to be a Christian is *to have to* suffer, that a sinner must be *humiliated by God* in order to be made righteous. Does speaking rightly about God today demand that we abandon the theologizing of bygone thinkers such as Martin Luther?

Feminist and other contemporary theologians proclaim that speaking rightly of God requires radical reform of traditional theologies like Luther's. That theology is contextual has become a central claim in current theological parlance, and Luther's own admonitions on wrath, sin, and guilt add real insult to real injury when spoken to those whose lives bear the marks of real crucifixions. Even more pointedly, traditional theories of atonement and theologies of the cross have come under attack by feminists and others who work to unmask these theologies' damage to the wounded, the vulnerable, and the oppressed. Where is the good news preached to the victimized? The responsibility for such oppression and suffering is being laid at the feet of the traditional Christian patriarchy, of which Luther is a card-carrying member. Cries for reform rise up, and they deserve a hearing.

But cries of reform also rose up over five hundred years ago from the mouth and pen of Luther over the oppressive theology and church practices of his own day. Theologians of his day, Luther proclaimed, had bypassed the cross of Christ. They were following instead glory theologies that traced disingenuous paths to God, paths controlled by religious decrees of the seemingly all-powerful medieval church. A theology of glory, according to Luther, declared salvation attainable through human effort, effectively painting a false picture of humanity's stance before God. Diametrically opposed to any theology of glory that called good evil and evil good, Luther glimpsed an alternate reality through the cross of Christ, an alternative vision of what counted as authority, wisdom, and salvation. While Luther is often critiqued for separating the material from the spiritual and thereby severing his theology from ethics, I argue that when his theology is investigated alongside his concrete attempts at living it, we find a Luther passionately concerned with the material condition of the peasants he viewed as oppressed by the corrupt ecclesial institution of the day. What Luther accomplished in his Reformation was nothing less than a new way of perceiving church, theology, and the Christian's role in society. By reasserting the cross's primacy in Christian speech and practice, Luther destabilized an entire tradition and attacked the institution that lay claim to the hearts, minds, and souls of medieval Christians.

Thus there exists a divide. Luther stands on one side; feminists and many other contemporary theologians stand on the other, separated not only by centuries but also by commitments. Here I stand, confessing allegiance to both Luther's cross-centered vision and to feminists' vision of theology free from debilitating sexism. As a female theologian trained in the late twentieth century, I credit my feminist predecessors for having given me voice, for fighting for my right to claim my identity as "theologian." My feminist foremothers opened doors to the future, allowing me to experience not only women in church pulpits but also a religious tradition confessing and slowly breaking from its legacy of harm against women and others outside its traditional hierarchy of power. At the same time, however, I continue to be claimed by my heritage as a Lutheran, raised on a theology of the cross that never lets me forget my chronic predisposition to sin, the inevitability of suffering, and God's saving work through the cross and resurrection of Christ. Is it possible to claim both feminism and Luther? Is the divide that separates them crossable?

Some days I wonder. The chasm gapes, yawns, and sometimes I fall in. Some days I encounter a Luther basking in his and others' sufferings in ways my feminist self rejects as masochistic. Other days I encounter feminist theologians who avoid women's own chronic predisposition to sin, which my Lutheran self cannot affirm. But on better days, I sense that I am not schizophrenic—that both Luther's visions for life with the cross at the center *and* feminist visions for Christian repentance and healing can be brought together in ways that preserve the integrity of both sides. Most of the time I meet in Luther a reformer who imagines a new form of Christian existence, free from the existentially (and, in subtler ways, materially) oppressive structures that became intolerable in late-medieval Christendom. Revisiting Luther's theology of the cross, feminists will be surprised to meet in Luther an ally in strategizing *how* theologians can reimagine and reform dominant, abusive versions of Christianity and render a more faithful, liberating portrait of life lived in response to the gospel message. Those who reside firmly on Luther's side also will learn more from feminists about the nightmarish realities of human suffering and about theology's role in the persistence of such unnecessary pain. With their gaze focused on the concrete experiences of women—particularly the suffering women whose lives bespeak a shattered existence, if indeed they survive at all—feminist theologians challenge traditional theological claims of sin, selfhood, suffering, and redemption. The divide can be crossed, and this text is an exercise in crossing and bridge-building.

This book is not primarily about atonement—that is, about *how* God reconciles the broken world back to God—although the topic cannot and will not be avoided. Feminist critiques regarding the abusive potential of atonement theories are weighty and deserve attention. But just as Luther exposes in his intimate portrait of human existence *coram Deo*, as standing before God, the cross is about more than theories. The cross is about the existential meeting—often a confrontation—between Christians and the suffering Christ on the cross. Luther's existential encounter remains significant because it gave rise to an unsentimental theology that radically destabilized the ecclesial, and subsequently the societal, status quo. But this is tricky, dangerous business. Human suffering is neither equal in scope nor univocal in meaning; in fact, some suffering defies any attempt to give it meaning. A feminist theology of the cross requires careful treatment of the types of human suffering, including a careful accounting of which forms are acceptable and which are not. Let us turn now to the task of this book itself.

Part one focuses on Luther. Since more has been written about Martin Luther than about virtually any other figure in the West (barring Jesus Christ!), I will say a word about what this treatment of Luther offers that others do not. The three chapters comprising part one offer a reading of Luther's theology of the cross indebted to Walther von Loewenich's argument that Luther's cross-centered approach remained integral to his lifelong career as a reformer.[1] I also am influenced by Gerhard Forde's recent rereading of Luther's *Heidelberg Disputation*, the seminal text for Luther's theology of the cross.[2] But as a feminist who takes seriously the claim that theology should be judged at least partly by its lived reality,[3] I stand with Douglas John Hall in his persistent call to see Luther's theology of the cross as contextual theology, both in Luther's time as well as in our own;[4] therefore I investigate Luther's theology in light of his involvement in social, political, and economic issues of his day. If Luther is to be viewed as a resource for contemporary theologians committed to contributing to actual transformation and healing, then we must assess how Luther's theology fared in its lived reality of the sixteenth century. This is what part one sets out to do.

Chapter 1 begins with an introduction to Luther's early theology, his stepping out as a theologian of the cross, and the initial ramifications of his new and critical approach. Chapter 2 examines how Luther's cross-centered vision became a tool for change as he sailed to his reformation heights of the early 1520s, shouting down the walls of a corrupt and exploitative church. But Luther's heights lie close to his depths; therefore chapter 2 also attends to Luther's support of the princes during the Peasants' War of 1525, assessing the relationship between this political stance and his theology of the cross. Chapter 3 addresses the mature Luther, who married, wrote voluminous lectures on Genesis, and continued fighting battles, some of which present an embarrassing contrast with the Luther of the early Reformation. But his increasing involvement in social and political issues—as well as his continuing biblical exegesis—deserve attention. While brilliant and imaginative in his theological vision and attempts to embody it, Luther's great accomplishments as a reformer are at times matched by his greatness as a sinner; he himself could not see the liberating implications of his theology of the cross.

Part two introduces feminist theology and the significance of the feminist reformation within contemporary theology. Because feminists and Luther possess a reforming sensibility, both sides of the divide share some common methodological commitments. After examining these, chapter 4 investigates three major points of contention between Luther and feminist theologians: the meaning of sin, the significance of Jesus's maleness, and the reality of God's atoning work in the cross of Christ. For each, the topic of suffering shapes the argument in a threefold fashion. For each point, we explore first a feminist critique, then an imagined conversation between feminists and Luther to clarify the existing divide, and finally a way forward that holds both Lutheran and feminist commitments in dialectical tension.

Chapter 5 bridges the divide by articulating a vision of what it means to become a feminist theologian of the cross. A feminist, cross-centered vision draws on biblical narratives used by Luther—Genesis and John—that offer descriptions of cruciform existence and how it can be transformed by the gift of hope through encountering the resurrected, crucified Christ. A feminist theologian of the cross is at once committed to calling crucified women what they are—victims—while also naming carefully the shifting status between victim and oppressor that exists within each human life. The chapter concludes with a vision of justified existence that embraces vocation in terms of friendship, exemplified by Jesus's friendship with those who followed him. To become a feminist theologian of the cross is to adopt an appreciative yet critical stance toward both Luther and feminists, utilizing what is most valuable and significant from each. This is how we cross the divide.

Two disclaimers are worth noting: First, even though this book unfolds more or less chronologically, it does not pretend to offer a comprehensive treatment of the reformer's life and thought. My interest in Luther's theology of the cross is in its daily expression throughout his life. Second, this project is not about Luther's views of women per se; rather, I intend to present Luther's theological vision in a way that encourages feminists and Luther scholars alike to regard it as a possibly surprising resource for contemporary—particularly feminist—theological reflection.

That this project begins with Luther may prove problematic for some readers. I may be accused of honoring the voice of tradition over the voices of women—particularly those who live or even die under the violent effects of cross-centered theologies. While I cannot easily dismiss such concerns, I remain convinced that a contemporary theology of the cross risks misrepresentation unless it flows from an empathetic reading that situates it within its original context. But this book is not an *apologia* for Luther; it does not merely seek to reclothe a late-medieval theologian to make him more acceptable to feminists. Rather, through this exploration of Luther's theology of the cross as it was preached and lived within a particular context, I hope to create a space where feminists committed to reforming the church and its theology can meet Luther and view him as a partial ally in the never-ending struggle against theologies of glory that call good evil and evil good.

Finally, I embarked on this project because as a white North American Lutheran feminist theologian, I struggle to hold opposing claims regarding the cross, suffering, liberation, and salvation in some sort of dynamic tension. I wrote this book with hope that it may be of use to others living with similar tensions. I offer a theological vision that is both embedded within a Christian confessional tradition and committed to speaking to the lives of those on that tradition's margins. May this vision of becoming a feminist theologian of the cross speak of a life-giving faith that cannot and will not avoid the terror of Good Friday before embracing the hope of Easter's dawn.

Part
One

I

Claiming the Cross

Experience alone makes a theologian.
—Martin Luther

In a packed hall in Heidelberg, Germany, his monastic brothers strained to catch a glimpse of the controversial Martinus Lutheri, who would boldly and publicly defend his new vision for theology and the church. That day in May 1518, Luther passionately expressed that vision: a theology that begins and ends at the foot of the cross of Christ. While some scholars link this "theology of the cross" primarily with Luther's early thought, I side with others who contend that Luther's cross-centered vision stands at the heart of his entire life and his vocation as a theologian. As Gerhard Ebeling states, "By the *theologia crucis* [Luther] does not mean a subsidiary theme or a special kind of theology, but the criterion and subject of all true theology: 'True theology and knowledge of God lies in the crucified Christ.'"[1] Proclaiming "true theology" was Luther's constant concern.

But how did this troubled, devout monk come to ignite a reformation that swept through Europe and massively altered medieval religious thought and practice? What was it about his theology of the cross that sparked and even compelled reform? Indeed, Luther offered a new way of imagining Christian existence.[2] He came to reject much of the worldview of late-medieval Christianity, pursuing instead an intensely experiential understanding of religion. Toward the end of his life, Luther explained it this way: "Not reading and speculation, but living, dying, and being condemned make a real theologian."[3] And from this new vision of Christian existence came a new vision for the church and even for society as well.

The imaginative world of this "real theologian" grew out of the intense connection Luther drew between the trials of faith and the lives of the characters inhabiting the biblical text. Luther approached Scripture with a freshness and dynamism that opened the Word of God up to the average person. Luther's passionate investment in the power of the Word to transform human existence served as the foundation for his new theological vision.

Let us turn now to Luther's earliest days as a monk and as an emerging scholar of the biblical text. By tracing the thoughts and actions that led to his public presentation of his theology of the cross, we gain a portrait of Luther not as a born agitator searching for a public platform, but as a pious Christian struggling mightily to live and act according to God's will. Faith in the God of the Bible, Luther eventually concluded, demanded a defiant stance not only against the religious leaders of his day and the institutions they shaped, but also against the theology undergirding medieval Christianity itself.

The Stirring of Luther's Theological Imagination

After receiving a university education in Erfurt and briefly immersing himself in the study of law, twenty-one-year-old Luther entered the order of Augustinian monks. This order was renowned for its strong academics and severe ascetic practices. Luther devoted himself wholeheartedly to both pursuits, filling his days with serious study and incessant confession of sin. Scholasticism—the dominant medieval approach to theology and philosophy, built on the logic of Aristotle and the writings of the early church fathers—was standard fare for monastic study, and thus for Luther. On his own time, however, Luther was drawn into the biblical text. There he repeatedly encountered, much to his terror, an angry God and a judgmental Christ. At the monastery he reportedly trembled before any image of Christ. In fact, Luther was "incapable of gazing at the crucified, because the image of the judge was imposed upon it; or the crucified was only an illustration of the excruciating punishment awaiting the sinner himself."[4] As a monk Luther tried desperately to live a godly life, but his conscience refused to let him believe that placating a judging Christ or a wrathful God was actually possible. Even ordination into the priesthood failed to alleviate this affliction of conscience, which he called *Anfechtung*.[5] Unfortunately for Luther, he found little solace in scholastic theology. Its practitioners seemed utterly unaware of the terror of *Anfechtung* that pervaded his own personal encounters with God.

While he found much scholastic theology lacking in existential insight, Luther nevertheless embraced aspects of other late-medieval schools of thought. Luther's early writings reveal that not only scholasticism but humanism—a critical intellectual movement in late-medieval Europe—shaped his approach to both Scripture and theology. At this stage in his career, Luther shared at least three convictions with the humanists. First, both insisted upon returning to Scripture itself—in its original languages—rather than to the interpretive tomes of *scholia*. Alister McGrath suggests that the humanist slogan "back to the sources" (*ad fontes*) signaled more than a simple return to ancient texts. It also represented "a call to return to the essential realities of human existence as reported in these literary sources."[6] Clearly, Luther could not have become the biblical scholar he became without building on the accomplishments of the scholastic tradition.[7] Nevertheless, he followed a humanist trend as he grew to rely more on his personal impressions and their intersections with the biblical text rather than on the *scholia* as his primary source for reflection.[8]

Second, Luther shared with humanists a wariness of the scholastic appetite for Aristotle and what he came to regard as an overly formulaic approach to theology. While many humanists preferred Cicero and other Latin writers to Aristotle, Luther favored the Bible above all other sources. In his inaugural lectures on the Psalms (1513–15), Luther relied predominantly on the *quadriga*, the accepted fourfold scholastic method of interpretation. Yet by the time he introduced his Augustinian brothers to his theology of the cross at Heidelberg, Luther had abandoned the *quadriga* and—as we shall see—many of scholasticism's fundamental assumptions along with it.

Third, one can argue that the humanist fascination with rhetorical eloquence influenced Luther's own exegetical and theological expression. While at times humanists regarded eloquence as an end in itself, Luther always intended for his rhetorical creativity to serve the preaching and proclaiming of God's Word.[9] Moreover, Luther captured the imaginations of average folk throughout Germany by speaking with an eloquence accessible to any and all Christians. "You must ask the mother at home, the children in the street and the common man in the marketplace, and see on their own lips how they speak, and translate accordingly, so that they understand it and realize that you are speaking German to them."[10] For Luther, writes Peter Matheson, "human speech itself was a sacrament."[11]

In many ways new and innovative, Luther's theology remained rooted in the intellectual soil of his day. His shared convictions with humanists did not go unnoticed by humanists themselves. In the early days of Reformation activity, humanists provided Luther critical support for his vision, thus bolstering his influence both within and outside the church. The young Luther was beginning a journey that was always much more than academic to him.

The Totally Other Face

At age twenty-nine, Luther received his doctorate in theology and joined the faculty at a relatively obscure university in Wittenberg. It was there, in his post as professor of biblical theology, that Luther would begin to envision a theological universe quite different from the one in which he had been raised. His early lectures on Psalms, Romans, and other biblical books propelled him more deeply into Scripture, where he began to glimpse something other than the God of the medieval portraits surrounding him. While steeped in the lament and praise of the Psalms, Luther encountered a poet whose writings bespoke the *Anfechtung* that Luther knew so well. The Psalmist's words not only spoke to his besieged conscience; Luther also heard them bear witness to the *Anfechtung* that pierced the suffering and dying Christ. Luther discovered a Psalmist who witnessed not only to Christ's battle with *Anfechtung* but also to his consistently humble response to such terror. The more Luther studied the biblical text, the more he became convinced that Scripture preached humility as the faithful response to all of life's trials and their accompanying *Anfechtung*. Indeed, Luther never shook his own experiences of *Anfechtung*. To the contrary, his terrified conscience inspired him to embrace a new theological vision, one that originated at the foot of the cross.

In his early interpretations of the Psalms, Luther employed the fourfold meaning of Scripture, but he altered the scholastic conventions. Infusing the process with his existential emphasis, Luther instead revived the Pauline distinction of the letter versus the spirit of the text, which, as Ebeling suggests, had come to be used very differently within medieval biblical interpretation. Luther, writes Ebeling,

> did not regard the literal meaning as such as the "letter that kills," and the allegorical, tropological, and anagogical interpretations elements of the fourfold method of interpretation imposed upon it as the "life-giving Spirit". Instead, he based the fundamental distinction between the letter that kills and the life-giving Spirit on the substance of what was expressed in the whole fourfold meaning of scripture. The whole can be the letter that kills, or the whole can be the life-giving Spirit, depending upon whether the understanding is oriented towards Moses or towards Christ.[12]

Luther's insistence that an entire Psalm can preach letter or spirit signaled his first significant break with medieval biblical interpretation. This letter/spirit distinction later gives way in Luther to the law/gospel dialectic, and it is here that Luther begins to grasp at a new imaginative universe. In his lectures on the Psalms, we see a Luther who strives to understand the Psalms as communicating more than mere letter. Immersed in the Psalter's laments, Luther discovers a text concerned with "Christ himself," finding in the Psalms the details of Christ's suffering, all the way to his experience of abandonment by God. It is through this immersion, Ebeling writes, that Luther prepares the way for his theology of the cross.[13]

Lecturing on Romans, Luther continued to push the traditional fourfold method to its breaking point. Throughout his lectures, Luther repeatedly grapples with an understanding of God's righteousness that seemed to counter prevailing scholastic views of the role of righteousness in one's relationship with God. For Luther, a crucial error for scholastic theologians was their appropriation of Aristotelian categories within the realm of grace. The problem was not that scholastics claimed that persons could become righteous before God *without* grace; for Luther the error involved the use of Aristotle's concept of *habitus*, or formation of an inner disposition, to claim that grace was imparted as an *inner quality*.[14] Why exactly did Luther believe it necessary to reject such an approach? The answer lies within his existential investment in interpreting the biblical text. Luther's own struggles with his conscience convinced him that a focus on human cooperation with God's righteousness only left one in a state of fear. "Have I done enough?" Luther would ask, petrified that he had not satisfied God's daunting expectations. While living in the monastery, Luther is said to have confessed his sins for hours at a time. Then, upon leaving the confessional, he would doubt his own sincerity and return for yet another attempt at complete confession. Toward the end of his life, Luther recalled these early days as a time not of loving God but of despising the one who would demand the impossible of sinners:

> As if, indeed, it is not enough that miserable sinners, eternally lost through original sin, are crushed by every kind of calamity by the law of the Decalogue, without having God add pain to pain by the gospel and also by the gospel threatening us with his righteousness and wrath.[15]

In Luther's mind, to speak of grace as something within is to assert that a person is justified only to the extent to which that grace is realized externally, within works.[16] To direct our gaze inward, toward the quality of the believer's inner life, left Luther with a God of whom he was terrified; he could do nothing other than hate the God he longed to love and serve.

The saving vision that struck Luther sometime in the second decade of the sixteenth century came through Paul's words to the Romans: "The righteous will live by faith" (Rom. 1:17). Luther's mentor Johann von Staupitz, then dean of the faculty at Wittenberg, encouraged him to see that Scripture ultimately testified to a more encompassing view of righteousness than he encountered in scholasticism.[17] Thus Luther came to hear anew these words in Romans—words that carved a path for him through God's terrifying wrath. It is from this Word of grace that Luther reenvisioned the church's doctrine of justification. No longer would he embrace the scholastic approach: that human beings must "do what is in them" *(quod in se est)* to achieve a status of worthiness before God. Instead Luther discovered through Paul a God whose righteousness comes to humanity not in the humanly expected form of punishment or reward, but as an undeserved gift given to sinners by grace. Luther writes in his lectures on Romans, "God does not want to redeem us through our own, but through external righteousness and wisdom, not through one that comes from us and grows in us, but through one that comes to us from the outside."[18] God justifies humanity not as a reward for humble living, as Luther initially feared, but rather through grace alone.

This gift of God's righteousness places the sinner, then, before God, clothed in divine righteousness. The magnitude of this realization for Luther cannot be underestimated: "I felt that I was altogether born again and had entered paradise itself through open gates. There a totally other face of the entire scripture showed itself to me."[19] This totally other face is neither remote nor even external; this face of Scripture dynamically engages the hearer, placing the believer *coram Deo.* Set free by this new insight, Luther was liberated from the problem of human attempts at justification before God. He embraced the vision he found in Paul: that the gospel reveals God's righteousness as rendering sinners righteous through Christ's death and resurrection.

Transformed by this new vision, Luther's views began to diverge more pointedly from those of both his predecessors and his contemporaries. Late-medieval scholastics interpreted the righteousness of Christ as ushering in a new law for Christians. For them, Christ replaced Moses not as redeemer but as lawgiver, and although Christ initiated the process of justification in the believer, the law still needed to be fulfilled. In this vision, God's righteousness remained distant, conferred upon sinners only after fulfillment of the new law. Luther's new vision of justification, however, was a radical departure. Grace does not equip human beings to become righteous; rather, the gift of grace fundamentally alters the situation for humanity *coram Deo*. Here we move into Luther's understanding of atonement in which, as Gerhard Forde says, Luther testifies not to what humanity gives to God, but rather to what God gives us through the death and resurrection of Christ.[20] Luther reasserts Christ's redemptive role, for *Christ himself* is the righteousness of God. Christ's life, death, and resurrection, Luther writes, guarantees "our own spiritual resurrection and life."[21] Rather than referring to the realm of pure spirituality, Luther uses the term "spiritual" to indicate "the category of true understanding," wherein living in the Spirit means to live in faith.[22] Consequently, our spiritual relationship to God's work in Christ is one of radical receptivity, where righteousness is received by us through the gift of grace. Luther makes an analogy: "The earth receives the rain in this way. It does not create it through any work, and cannot obtain water through any work of its own, but it receives the rain. As much as the rain is the earth's own, Christian righteousness is our 'own.'"[23] Luther proclaims that the rain of righteousness sinks into sinners. Therefore Luther counsels sinners to "believe at least your own experience," for by the law you deserve the wrath of God, but by grace you have been saved through faith.[24] This "totally other face of scripture" caught Luther in its gaze and never let him go.

But even though the rain of righteousness drenches the sinner, Luther is clear that the sin is not erased. The Christian's status as simultaneously justified and sinful *(simul justus et peccator)* indicates that justification, although efficacious in the present, does not lead to an idyllic existence. To be justified by God means to share in Christ's sufferings and subsequently in the afflicting *Anfechtung.* "To be a Christian," Luther writes, "is to have to suffer."[25] As Mary Solberg suggests, Luther's focus on a suffering existence is not intended as a condemnation of humanity. Instead Luther was "passionately concerned to describe the situation in which humans are"—whether they know it or not.[26] Speaking descriptively, Luther knew that living as a Christian leads *into* the wilderness before leading out of it. Even though Luther admitted he did not "understand this mystery fully,"[27] he knew he had been transformed by his encounter with the Word of God's saving work in Scripture. Only through God's work in Christ on the cross do human beings receive new life and stand justified before God. This good news must be preached by way of the cross. Here we begin to see how the cross becomes central to Luther's proclamation of justification and salvation.

New Language for a New Vision

Luther found some elements of mystical imagery compelling, and he incorporated them into his vision of faithful living in response to the cross of Christ. He kept his distance from mystical visions of union with Christ in which the divine/human distinction is obliterated, but gravitated toward the language and imagery of the mystic John Tauler, praising his writings for their "wisdom based on experience rather than theory."[28] Tauler spoke of the inevitability of suffering and *Anfechtung* in a life of faith, striking a resonant chord with Luther. Along with biblical writers such as the Psalmist, Tauler and other mystical writers "taught Luther the language of spiritual devotion."[29] Transcending more reasoned scholastic discussion, their imagery opened up for Luther a deeper existential dimension of the relationship between the believer and the resurrected crucified Christ.

It should come as no surprise, then, that Luther incorporated mystical elements into the syntax and style of his theological vocabulary. Just as the mystics regarded darkness as a potentially fruitful breeding ground for spiritual insight, so Luther envisioned faith as necessarily existing in darkness. Where faith is, Luther said, there is "night in the intellect."[30] In the dark night of faith Christians come to trust a God largely unknown and hidden from view. Luther's mystical imagery leads to the cross, where God remains clothed in the humanity of Christ—an image found at the heart of his theology of the cross. The God of the cross works glory on the believer's spirit, Luther proclaims, while on the outside "everything appears as its opposite."[31] The spiritual union between the believer and Christ first entails the terrifying experience of God's negation of all human striving. Only then can the believer be justified. While righteousness comes to us externally, it takes hold of the believer, becoming incarnate in the believer's life and being. As Erwin Iserloh suggests, "If we understand clearly that 'ontological' does not equal something reified, material, and static, then we should not hesitate to speak of an ontological transformation."[32] Receiving the gift of righteousness ignites a mystical, spiritual transformation of the life of the believer.

But while union with Christ played a vital role in Luther's new vision, the mystical concept of imitating Christ did not. Of critical importance to Luther's vision of salvation by faith alone is the "once for all" character of God's atoning work in Christ. Later Luther came to call what happened on the cross a "joyous exchange" *(fröhliche Wechsel)* between God and humanity. In Christ's taking in of human sinfulness through suffering and death, justification is accomplished by God and offered to us as a gift, albeit one that is hidden in the sufferings of the cross. Luther called the exchange joyous precisely because justification comes as a sheer gift. Therefore he vigorously rejected the language of imitation, and along with it any indication that human work can succeed in achieving any kind of righteous status before God. For Luther, unification with Christ's righteousness comes not from the strivings of imitation toward moral perfection—but from receiving a gift while gripped by sin.

While the mystics provided language and images for Luther, his new vision was linked most profoundly to his reading of Scripture. The established fourfold approach to Scripture ultimately failed Luther because he could not see how the method allowed the spirit of the text to emerge in living, dynamic, and existentially compelling ways. Rejecting what he viewed as a formulaic reading, Luther seized on what he called the "literal" sense of Scripture: it sets the power of God's Word free to transform the hearer. Ebeling describes Luther's embrace of this understanding of God's Word as the decisive proclamation about human existence.

> The less one approaches the scripture from a previously established position, looking for specific answers to specific questions . . . and the more radically one accepts the challenge to one's own existential life of an encounter with scripture, concentrating upon a single fundamental question aimed at human existence itself and touching one's very conscience, the more one looks ultimately for only one thing in scripture, the word which brings certainty in life and in death . . .[33]

The one thing in Scripture—that with which the literal sense is preoccupied—is the promise of Christ, present not only in the passion narratives, but "everywhere in scripture."[34] We glimpse an emerging vision in which Luther can claim "the cross alone is our theology."[35]

It is precisely in Luther's move to the cross that the force of his understanding of the gospel comes to the fore. And his biblical interpretation relies explicitly upon his understanding of faith. In faith, the truth about the cross of Christ—exemplified for Luther in the Romans passage "the righteous will live by faith"—becomes for Luther the "truth of the heart."[36] By emphasizing the externality of the Word, Luther avoids a "'truth as subjectivity' in the superficial sense that faith is true when it is subjectively heartfelt."[37] Rather, through faith, the truth of what God accomplished through the cross of Christ creates a "decisive change in the self."[38] This encounter with God's Word through Scripture does not prescribe specific moral action, but creates a new relationship with God based on faith. To live in light of the claim that the "righteous will live by faith," then, does not translate into conformity with particular requirements; instead it involves accepting the "gift" character of human existence.

Initial Controversies

It was only a matter of time before Luther's new vision pushed him to publicly oppose the prevailing views of his day. In 1517 Luther crafted his *Disputation Against Scholastic Theology*, in which he protested many major tenets of scholasticism. Even though Luther continued to use the methods of disputation—the scholastic framework for debate—he vigorously rejected scholasticism's approach to theology. Most grievous was scholasticism's wedding of Aristotelian categories to the doctrine of grace, which, Luther believed, resulted in a dismissal of the idea of grace as definitive for Christian existence. Luther accused scholastics of Pelagianism—of believing that persons are capable of achieving salvation through their own moral effort. For Luther insisted that there is "no moral virtue without sin" (thesis 38). Convinced that divine righteousness alone bestows salvation, Luther balked at the scholastic notion that "one can do what one has the power and ability to do" through internal cooperation with God's gift of grace. Luther accused the scholastics of deceiving Christians: "I have learned nothing [from the scholastics] but the ignorance of sin, righteousness, baptism, and the whole of Christian life. I certainly didn't learn there what the power of God is. . . . Indeed, I lost Christ there, but I have found him again in Paul."[39] Equipped with his new interpretation of God's Word, Luther spoke out, calling the church and the academy away from Aristotle and back to the encounter with God through the Word.

While this university professor participated in academic debates and reform movements emerging within his own university, Luther simultaneously harbored suspicion for those Christians who limit themselves to a life of study: "Great scholars who read much and abound in books are not the best Christians," he wrote.[40] For Luther the pastor, questions of righteousness and faith extended far beyond the classroom walls, even—much to the dismay of Rome—to church practices such as indulgences.

The medieval church sold indulgences to laypersons, offering them reassurance that their debt of sin would be paid. In 1517 Luther presented to the church the now-famous Ninety-five Theses, in which he interrogated what had become a highly suspect church practice. To Luther, the insidiousness of indulgences lay in their implicit claim that righteousness could be bought, which effectively nullified its character as a sheer gift from God through Christ's suffering and death on the cross. And if degrading the holy role of Christ was not enough, Luther accused the papacy of robbing the peasants who bought indulgences in order to secretly fund the great basilicas in Rome (theses 43, 45, 46). To Luther's disgust, indulgences seemed to mislead parishioners just as scholasticism misled theologians: they both intimated that salvation depended at least in part on human acts of righteousness. Luther could hold his silence no longer, and raised his voice against this assault on the power of God.

Until the publication of his attack on indulgences, Luther had been a relatively obscure monk teaching at an insignificant though reform-minded university. With his bold critiques, especially those leveled against established church practice, Luther catapulted himself "into fame among sympathizers and infamy among opponents."[41] Rather than backing away from the public arena and allowing the dust to settle, Luther continued proclaiming his new theological vision to an ever-widening circle of hearers. The Augustinian order offered Luther his next occasion for a public accounting, in Heidelberg, where Luther emerged as a theologian of the cross.

Stepping Out as a Theologian of the Cross

When he appeared before his Augustinian brothers in the spring of 1518, Luther knew his writings were generating controversy near and far. His attacks on scholastic theology caused waves among church leaders, while his irreverent attitude toward indulgences fueled fires of protest among lay Christians throughout Germany. Shortly before his appearance in Heidelberg, the Dominicans in Rome formally denounced Luther's teachings. Intending to quell this voice of protest before it could ignite further unrest, Luther's superiors called the meeting in Heidelberg, hoping they could address and contain Luther's critiques within the fold.[42]

Unfortunately for his superiors, this strategy backfired. Luther presided over the discussion of his *Disputation* (which he was ordered to write for the occasion), capturing the imaginations of those who witnessed his performance. Shortly thereafter, his *Heidelberg Disputation* was published and distributed, heightening Luther's exposure and emerging celebrity status. What was it about this scholarly defense that captured the minds and hearts of so many people who encountered it? At Heidelberg, Luther presented a compellingly new vision for theology and the task of the theologian. Using evocative biblical metaphors and images, Luther retold the story of human experience in light of Christ's cross and resurrection.[43] He then starkly contrasted his theology of the cross with what he argued was a perennially deceptive theology of glory. For Luther, no faithful compromise between the two approaches existed. Either one occupied the faithful stance of a theologian of the cross or relegated oneself to the unfaithful stance of a theologian of glory.

As Ebeling notes, Luther built his thought around antitheses, around tensions between strongly opposed yet related polarities.[44] Theology, Luther believed, entails witnessing to the relationship between humanity and the God who governs all distinctions. Due to our chronic predisposition to sin, however, human beings experience the world in paradoxical terms. Negotiating these paradoxes cannot follow uncritically from the church and its decrees, Luther declared, but only from God's alien and proper work in the cross of Christ. For Luther, "theology as the object of intellectual inquiry and theology as the sphere of a personal encounter formed an indivisible unity."[45] Luther's *Disputation* not only attacks the theological and ecclesial status quo, but also offers a stark alternative vision of the theologian before God.

Inquiry and Encounter

Undoubtedly his superiors expected Luther's disputation to set forth basic doctrinal claims that could be debated and countered. Luther did follow the disputational format, but, as Gerhard Forde observes, he did not present a doctrine of the cross.[46] It goes without saying that Luther regarded christological claims as worthy of serious reflection, yet he intended his theology of the cross to extend far beyond academic debate to the arena of personal experience and divine encounter. What Luther accomplished at Heidelberg was to describe how a theologian of the cross operates in the world in response to the transforming power of the cross.[47]

The overarching vision for a cross theologian emerges from the imagistic world of the Bible that Luther inhabited as he taught and preached. For Luther, as we have seen, Scripture's light was less a doctrinal source than an active world of patriarchs, prophets, psalmists, and apostles that erupted into and shaped the Christian's life.[48] At Heidelberg Luther testified to such eruption as he rendered an account of a theologian living among such biblical images, all of which he read as pointing to the cross. Although Luther introduced his theology of the cross in an academic forum, his theological vision becomes meaningless unless the cross event becomes the "truth of the heart" to which Christians live in response. Thus it was not a doctrine of the cross that occupied Luther at Heidelberg, but a passionate drive to describe what it means to live *coram Deo* before a crucified God.

We cannot ignore the fact that Luther's own personal struggles to understand the proper relationship between God and human beings

fueled his primarily pastoral orientation toward theology. As Rowan
Williams suggests, Luther decisively reinstated experience as a theologically significant matter.[49] It is through experience that one comes to know
God as the one hidden in the suffering of Christ.[50] But what does the conviction that "the cross alone is our theology" mean for Christian existence? The *Disputation* tells the story of what the cross does to the sinful
self, a story that results in despair. We must not forget, however, that for
Luther the cross ultimately heralds good news for the Christian because it
is out of the cross that God works resurrection. Indeed, the expressions of
hope and joy with which Luther concludes the *Disputation* are possible only
if Christians view the cross through the lens of the resurrection.

Describing the Human Condition

The conventional approach to sketching out Luther's cross theology
involves focusing on select theses of the *Disputation* (particularly theses
19, 20, 21, and 24) wherein Luther explicitly uses the phrase "theologian (or theology) of the cross." Forde warns, however, that glossing over
the first eighteen theses can prevent readers from comprehending the full
import of Luther's theological vision. For Luther, union with Christ
meant that one experiences what Christ experienced. Before there can be
a resurrection, then, there must be a death.[51] Theses 1 through 18 offer a
portrait of how the cross brings low the sinful self. Luther describes the
ensuing existential crisis in feverish terms in thesis 18, declaring, "It is
certain that man must utterly despair of his own ability before he is pre-
pared to receive the grace of Christ." A theologian of the cross must first
attend to the despair brought about by experiencing what Luther calls
"God's alien work in the cross" before celebrating the new life offered in
the resurrected Christ.

How is the sinful self humbled before God? Luther tells the story
of how human beings, in their many efforts to become righteous,
accomplish nothing other than the creation of a false, deceptive vision
of reality. Throughout the first half of the *Disputation*, Luther peels away
layer after layer of illusion, demonstrating how every possible avenue of
human effort fails to achieve righteousness before God. He begins by
exposing how sinful human beings can never fulfill the law. Luther then

shows how the law is based on the illusion of the effectiveness of good works, and he concludes that trust in good works springs from yet another illusion: a will free to choose the good. Where does this chain of illusion lead? On the one hand, the chain causes Christians to utterly despair of their own efforts to attain righteousness (thesis 18). On the other, only when one has descended to the depths of despair can one hear the Word of hope. Let us travel with Luther the path that leads to despair and opens up to hope.

The story begins with the clash between God's righteousness and the law. Luther quotes Paul in Romans 3:2, "But now the righteousness of God has been manifested apart from the law" (thesis 1). What exactly is the law? For Luther, it is not a collection of dead commands, but "a living reality that is universally embodied in the threatening demands" of authorities in every facet of life.[52] In light of the controversies of his day, Luther stressed that works of law are "those which are regarded in themselves as being self-sufficient for righteousness and salvation."[53] Rather than functioning as a template for the pursuit of righteousness, the law instead serves a negative purpose: it exposes sin. Paul calls the law a law of death because it stands as judge over all human efforts to fulfill it (Rom. 8:2, thesis 1). But theologians of the day took their first step along the path of delusion, Luther argued, when they refused to accept the verdict Paul renders on the law, and continued to speak of the law as guidance for godliness.

Misplaced trust in the law builds upon a prior conviction that good works are not only possible, but also somehow meritorious when it comes to salvation. As his saving encounter with God's Word taught Luther, moving toward God through inner moral effort—however strenuous or well intentioned—is ultimately doomed to failure. As he says in theses 3 and 4, the outwardly attractive appearance of earnest human works constantly tempts the believer to trust their goodness and effectiveness. But appearances can deceive. A theologian of the cross resists this temptation and instead is humbled and frightened by the law and by the sight of his or her sin, realizing that even one's best efforts at faithful living are damaged by sin (thesis 4). To swell with pride over good works is to commit idolatry. In the face of such temptation, a theologian of the cross counsels humility. Humility for Luther, we must remember, is not merely a human technique for approaching God. Luther talks of any humbling of the self in passive rather than active terms. The depth and pervasiveness of their sinfulness leaves human beings turned in upon themselves *(incurvatus in se)*. Being brought low by the cross is *to be humbled* through God's alien work.

But what exactly does it mean to be, as Luther puts it, "humiliated by God"? How are we to make sense of this "scary vocabulary"? At this point in his career, Luther had not yet explicitly articulated his view on the two kingdoms; nevertheless, this later distinction can help us interpret the meaning of "passivity" with respect to his theology of the cross. Put simply, humanity's fundamental situation is defined by its existence before God *(coram Deo)* and, secondarily, by its existence before others in society *(coram hominibus)*. Living before God defines one's spiritual existence; here the state of the conscience and soul matters most. In the temporal realm where one lives with others, flesh and "activities of the flesh" take center stage. While some regard Luther's distinction as dualistic, Lewis Spitz and others argue that instead of viewing the spirit as serving God and the flesh as serving the world, Luther understood "one and the same [person]" as inhabiting both realms.[54] Applying this idea to passivity, "being humiliated" is a work God does to us rather than a work we do to ourselves. This act of God is none other than an attack on the sin residing within the sinful self. Far from indicating personal disengagement, Luther envisions passivity as a stance of total receptivity before God,[55] where personal will, private agendas, and desire no longer cloud one's relationship with God. Once the sinful gaze inward is shattered, Luther asserts, one's passive aptitude for a righteous spiritual life can be filled, through grace, with God's righteousness. Before others in society *(coram hominibus)*, one then becomes utterly receptive to the needs and wounds of the neighbor. Spiritual humiliation, then, sets believers free for faithful living outwardly focused on *active* service to God.

Luther's preoccupation with passivity continues into thesis 14, where he gets to the heart of the matter: the power to do good *coram Deo* exists only in a passive capacity. For Luther, the deepest level of illusion is the most difficult to unmask: the belief in free will. The theologian of the cross tells the story of humanity after the fall, with free will existing in name only (thesis 13). For Luther, the will stands at a critical juncture of separation between cross theologians and glory theologians, for glory theologians, Luther insists, always assert that the will is in control.[56] Because sin pervades the will, and because righteousness comes to us only from without, Luther speaks of the will as possessing only a "passive aptitude" for righteous existence in the spiritual realm.[57] Here the account comes full circle: Christians recognize their sinfulness when they encounter the accusation that comes through the law, God's tool of judgment. The preaching of the law shows "what we have failed to do and how much we have to do."[58] The will, infested with sin, is incapable of cooperating inwardly with God's gift of grace. In light of Luther's dialectical understanding of human existence, it becomes clear that the law does not ask human beings to inflict pain upon themselves. Instead, humans experience the active function of the law to humble them and awake a sense of despair about any human effort to work out one's own salvation (cf. thesis 18).

To encounter the law is to become entangled with humility and suffering. To be humbled by God, Luther insists, is to be "emptied through suffering [cf. Phil. 2:7]" (thesis 24). For Luther, this suffering is intimately related to his understanding of *Anfechtung*, suggesting that the affliction is "not just or even primarily physical," but an affliction of conscience.[59] When suffering is viewed through Luther's dualistic lens, the pain and suffering discussed within a theology of the cross are first and foremost by-products of the internal struggle needed to empty ourselves of all aspirations to heal ourselves, or to make ourselves righteous. We want to be in control. We want to do it ourselves. The message of the theology of the cross is that we cannot do it. We cannot vanquish sin. Where, then, are we to turn?

Many in Luther's day turned to the church. If we return to Luther's attack on the church practice of indulgences, we see that, in his view, the church appeared to advertise them as a cure for spiritual suffering. The type of suffering with which Luther was most preoccupied *was* the spiritual kind; therefore, any temporal remedy—such as a written grant of an indulgence—was, for Luther, nothing more than smoke and mirrors. The suffering that concerned Luther most—that which results from humanity's broken relationship with God—can be efficaciously addressed by God alone. It becomes apparent that Luther's bifurcation of the spiritual and the material realms is essential to his theology of the cross. Much to the dismay of theologians of glory, then, every possible human avenue toward righteousness is cut off: one cannot fulfill the law; one cannot even perform a good work without sinning; and one cannot choose freely that which is pleasing to God.

Confronted with this dead end, Luther anticipates the question, "What then shall we do?" (thesis 16). In the same thesis he assures his hearers, "The law makes us aware of sin so that, having recognized our sin, we may seek and receive grace." Knowing the depth of one's sinfulness leads one into hell, into the utter despair that comes with sinking into this spiritual quicksand. And yet—and here is the pastoral concern—theology must speak to the believer's existential situation. And only now, when every path of self-help is cut off, when anxiety over the failure of self-improvement techniques has set in—only then can hope begin to be preached. Thus, "Not despair but hope is preached when we're told we're sinners" (thesis 17). This is the point where theology begins. It is only in the depths of the godless world most extreme that all speculation, all hopes of self-sufficiency, fall away.[60]

Read one way, Luther is relating a highly personal, experiential story about sinners encountering the cross of Christ, being judged for creating illusions that we think will save us from being damned by our own failures. Read on another level, however, Luther's theology of the cross tells a more public, corporate story about how intellectual inquiry into humanity's relationship with God cannot only mislead the imagination, but also can create a fictitious universe in which ecclesial institutions come to practice a theology of glory that is tricked by appearances. The alternative story Luther wants to tell is one in which human beings live within their limits, understanding the cross as the meeting place between a sinful humanity and a saving God.

Living within the Limits

In the theses most commonly addressed in treatments of Luther's cross theology (19 through 21, 24), he posits two diametrically opposed visions of reality: one that invests in the outward appearances of human

and institutional work and one that insists that such appearances ultimately deceive, and that reality is hidden *sub contrario*, under its opposite.
Being attracted to outward appearances is but half the error, for "that
person does not deserve to be called a theologian who looks upon the
invisible things of God as though they were clearly perceptible" (thesis
19). Luther relies here on Paul's depiction in Romans 1 of the Gentiles
as "fools" because they may "know God" through a kind of natural theology, but fail to "honor and thank God." Luther likens the scholastic
theologians of glory to the fools of Paul's time in their failure to see that
knowing those "invisible things of God" is not decisive for faith. In other
words, affirmations of God's omnipotence or omnipresence are of little
value for the sinner standing *coram Deo*. When it comes to the value of
reason and philosophy *coram Deo*, Luther has already made the point that
all such avenues are cut off. This is not to say that reason and philosophy
are useless to Luther (cf. thesis 24). On the contrary. In the earthly realm,
applied to temporal issues, Luther believes reason and philosophy to be
precious gifts. But before God, reason offers nothing but darkness.[61]
When confronted by the Word of God spoken through the cross, Luther
declares, a theologian sees a God who "overthrows speculative theology
by making himself a *worldly* reality."[62] A theology of the cross takes its
"measure from the crucifixion and is characterized by limiting itself to
this world, God's coming to [us], [God's] giving and [our] receiving, low-
liness, living within the limits of humanity in the consciousness of living
coram Deo, in the presence of God."[63] While glory theologians speculate
over God's imperceptible majesty, cross theologians remain earthbound,
in the presence of God, at the foot of the cross.

To address the imperceptibility of God, Luther speaks about the hidden character of God's revelation in Christ. Cross theologians readily admit
that God's revelation comes to humanity highly mediated. Seeing the revelation of the hidden God *(Deus absconditus)* is central to seeing how God
operates with human beings. The apostle Paul admits that the message of
the cross appears to the unfaithful as sheer foolishness, but appears as the
power of God to those who are being saved (1 Cor. 1:18). So, too, Luther
highlights the hidden character of God clothed in Christ. Precisely where
God seems least likely to be—in the shocking, shameful event of the
cross—there God is, "hidden in the suffering." God's revelation is hidden

sub contrario, that is, hidden within God's own strange and alien work. Embracing such a vision of God can only be done from the perspective of faith—but faith, for the theologian of the cross, is also hidden from view *coram hominibus.* For cross theologians, then, God's double way of operating is subversive in the same way a theology of the cross is subversive: the affirmation can be seen only as hiding within the negation.

What is at stake in operating as a cross or glory theologian, according to Luther, is nothing less than an accurate representation of reality. Just as the prophet Isaiah admonishes the Israelite leadership for deceiving the people in Isaiah 5:20, so too does Luther accuse theologians of glory of calling evil good and good evil, while a theologian of the cross calls the thing what it is (thesis 21). A theologian of the cross, in stark contrast to a theologian of glory, sees the story of despair told through earlier theses as the result of God's strange work toward the sinner. As Isaiah declared, God's strange work is precisely what humbles sinful human beings (Isa. 28:21). Luther's terrifying bouts of *Anfechtung* betray how frightening he knew this strange work to be. The God of the cross is a God who hates sin, judging and condemning it through the cross, and thereby also in the life of each and every Christian. The resulting death is a real one; it is a death to every ounce of trust in one's own self-sufficiency, in any hoped-for ability to help orchestrate one's own liberation from sin.

The life-saving message of grace comes precisely because the strange work is enacted on behalf of human beings, rather than against them.[64] God's wrath continually battles sinfulness as manifest in every person, and this is why *Anfechtung* fails to disappear. To call a thing what it is involves naming the spiritual despair that arises from one's inability to make oneself righteous before God. God continues to deflate the sinner's inflated sense of self by means of the terrifying image of the cross. As Williams writes, human knowledge of God is not like a subject's conceptual grasp of an object. For cross theologians, God is known only in and by the exercise of crucifying compassion: "If we are like him in that, we know him."[65] When Christians view their condition through the awful reality of the cross, God appears first as judge, but ultimately God, with compassion, breaks through the suffering as one who stands *for* us, and we see that the wrath is penultimate. After God's strange work comes God's proper work of bestowing grace on the believer. The theologian of the cross understands the subversive, hidden way in which God works and accepts it on faith.

Luther continues to attack theologians of glory, this time for avoiding an encounter with the cross, and subsequently for distorting biblical teachings and bypassing the accompanying existential experience of despair for the believer. As Douglas John Hall suggests, the theology of glory is misleading in its silencing of doubt.[66] In refusing to wrestle with the aesthetically unappealing realities of the cross, theologians of glory end up denying God's alien activity.[67] Luther faults glory theologians of his day for lingering over the seductive portrait of the majestic God, divorced from the ugly, messy business of human suffering. "They all want to imitate the form of God in Christ and not the form of a servant. . . . They want to reign with Christ," Luther writes.[68] For Luther, the sale of indulgences was just one example of the glory theologians' attempts to reign with Christ, and even—as he later charged—to unseat Christ. To take this route, Luther warns, only means that "Everyone who drinks of this water will thirst again" (John 4:13, thesis 22). Acquiring wisdom, power, or authority will not satiate the desire of the glory theologians. The only remedy for desire, Luther insists, is to extinguish it.

But the desire to know more, accumulate more, is a constant temptation. To emphasize this point, Luther invokes the biblical image of Moses' encounter with God in Exodus 33. Moses hears that he cannot see the face of God and live, so it is God's backside, rather than God's face, that encounters humanity. "The back of Christ is his humanity . . . and his divinity is his face."[69] Cross theologians, admitting the limits of language and sight *coram Deo*, are conscious that theological talk is always "backside" talk about God. But this is not as easy to accept as one might think. Luther's choice of Moses is instructive, for even Moses has aspirations of a theologian of glory, desiring to meet God face-to-face.[70] True humiliation *coram Deo* occurs when the relentless desire to "reign with Christ" has been blotted out. Only then can true faith and hope reside.

This tension between the back and the face, between God hidden and revealed, between desire and naked trust, is indicative of Luther's vision of human existence as lived paradox. On the one hand, Luther insists that theologians of the cross must stick to what is visible, namely, to the cross of Christ. On the other hand, Luther depicts Christian faith as trust in what believers cannot see: the hiddenness of God or the backside of Christ. The cross, while visible, bears God's hidden presence. God is revealed to human beings through the cross, yet that revelation remains veiled and mysterious; faith experiences it in darkness. As H. Jackson Forstman writes, Luther "understood what it means to be human, to see and not to see at the same time."[71] According to a theologian of the cross, faith does not equip one with perfect vision. Being made righteous by God allows Christians to experience God's proper work on their behalf. There are no blueprints, no requirements in the gospel for a life of faith. For Luther, faith does not make gods out of human beings; instead, it makes us truly human.[72]

The Hidden Victory of the Cross

In speaking rightly of faith, then, cross theologians point to the experience of being accused by the cross as the real beginning of faith. They must acknowledge what the cross realistically portrays: a God immersed in what is deemed base and ugly by the glory theology of the day. But we must not give the impression that the cross simply functioned as a symbol of realism for Luther. To be sure, Christ's death on the cross carried salvific meaning for Luther. Nevertheless, Luther remained relatively unconcerned with a systematic articulation of the what and how of God's saving work through Christ. For such a task, in the end, exceeds comprehension.[73]

It is surprising to realize that the theology of the cross stands as an indirect critique of various theories of atonement. When one finds oneself in a state of despair, "atonement theories do little good" for one's shattered existence.[74] Theoretical explanations do not eradicate the experience of judgment and wrath. The cross for Luther is more mirror-like than it is theoretical, and in this mirror "our line of sight is bent back upon itself, upon ourselves and our world."[75] The cross illumines for us both the harsh truth of condemnation and the gift of righteousness freely granted. Luther's theology of the cross has more to say about human existence in light of the cross than it does about the crucifixion event itself.

All this is not to say that Luther ignores atonement altogether. The significance of Luther's view of atonement lies in the dramatic conflict it depicts between God and the devil, wrath and grace, righteousness and sin.[76] This drama, Forde argues, is more true to actual experience of "living, dying, and being condemned." The drama features Christ, who, as the embodiment of God, actually dies under the curse of the law. For Luther, God's undergoing of the passion, the endurance of the consequence of the sins of others, cost God mightily. While Christ's life involved "the active doing of the law,"[77] Christ's death is not an active offering, but a passive suffering of the reality of sin and death in the world. To say that Christ justifies us, Gustav Aulen states, "is the same as saying Christ conquered sin, death, and the everlasting curse."[78] While Aulen's formulation is not the only way Luther understood atonement, it was a significant one. With the "tyrants" (as Luther called them) conquered, human freedom from bondage to sin, death, and the law becomes possible. With the aid of this image, Luther's exegesis could now reinstate the resurrection as intrinsically important to the work of Christ, whereas medieval theories stressing sacrifice or satisfaction remained limited to Good Friday as the primary or even sole locus of Christ's redemptive work.[79] In order for the crucifixion to be truly good news, the theologian of the cross testifies, it must be viewed from the other side of the resurrection. The final theses of the *Heidelberg Disputation* take us to that other side.

Born Anew

"To be born anew, we must first die and be raised up" (thesis 24). After ushering his hearers through the death of the old sinful self, Luther concludes his *Disputation* with the gospel message of resurrection, a reality that sparks hope in God's power to defeat sin and offer new life. But when calling the resurrection what it is, Luther is careful to explain its reality as hidden from view within our broken world. To live in the light of the resurrection does not equal reigning with Christ, as appealing as that may sound. Cross theologians understand Christian existence as one defined simultaneously by justification *and* sin. The life of faith is defined by constant movement from cross to resurrection and back again, from condemnation to justification and back. The resurrection reality of God's

triumph over sin and death must become, as Luther insisted, the truth of
the heart. It is a spiritual reality that is not yet materially visible. The
Christian hope is that in the midst of the messiness, brokenness, and
fleeting joys of this life, believers live, move, and have their being in the
proclamation that salvation has been won.

How, then, does a theologian of the cross live in the light of the resurrection? Cross theologians understand that it is not works that make
sinners righteous, but it is "righteousness [that] creates works" (thesis
25). On the resurrection side of the cross, Christians experience a breaking of the inward gaze upon the self, allowing them to turn outward
toward God and others in the world. The radical freedom from consum-
ing self-preoccupation opens one to seeing Christ in a fuller light. From
the perspective of faith, from the other side of the resurrection, Christians can now hear the words from Ephesians 5—"Be imitators of
God"—not as a requirement for righteousness, but as a "stimulant" for
loving action in the world (cf. thesis 27). As William Lazareth says of
Luther's vision, "As one's being precedes one's doing, so Christ as 'gift'
first nourishes your faith and makes you a Christian. Then second, Christ
as 'example' also exercises your loving service to your neighbor."[80] True
faith is manifest in the same crucifying compassion of Christ's work in
the world.

By examining the *Heidelberg Disputation* in its entirety, we are introduced to Luther's vision of how a cross theologian operates within the
limits of the knowledge of God and God's will for humanity to what can
be seen and understood through the cross. Luther's cross theology bears
witness to a version of Christian spirituality which holds that "in the
middle of the fire we are healed and restored, though never taken out of
it."[81] The cross is our theology, and that vision offers hope in the midst
of the fire.

* * * * *

This chapter has focused on the troubled monk who struggled within
his late-medieval confines and stepped out to publicly confess the saving
reality of God's earthly presence in the cross of Christ. Luther's image
of Christ was transformed from one of terror into one of joyous assurance: God's proper work of justification comes through God's strange

work of condemning the sin that infests human existence. Having confessed as a theologian of the cross over against the papal and scholastic theologian of glory, Luther called glory theologians to account for their disingenuous theology and oppressive practices. This cross/glory distinction is a hallmark of any theology of the cross, and it offends those theologians of glory who try to claim that God is anywhere other than hidden *sub contrario*, "under the opposite." God is on the cross, in the suffering of human existence, rather than with the powerful of medieval Christendom.

We turn now to the points of intersection between Luther's theology and the context in which he lived. What exactly does new life in Christ look like in Luther's own life? At Heidelberg, Luther stepped out of the known world of medieval Christendom and into a world that was beginning to turn upside down.

The Walls
Come Tumbling Down

The whole world is shaken and shattered on account of God's Word.
—Martin Luther, *On the Bondage of the Will*

L uther's encounters with God's Word were shattering experiences. Indeed, his theology of the cross witnesses to the shattering of the sinful self—an event that works its way out to the exterior world where the theologian of the cross calls to account those theologians of glory who wish to avoid such unpleasantries. In Luther's day, the shattering of the old, the glorified, the powerful was the only way for sinful humanity to glimpse God's presence hidden in the sufferings and clothed in the flesh of Christ.

Even though the exact phrase *theologia crucis* fades from his later writings, Luther remained convinced that only those who bear witness to Christ's death through the cross and to the new life possible in him deserve the title of theologian. After Heidelberg, Luther expanded his attacks on theologians of glory to include the papacy and even left-wing reformers who called for armed rebellion to usher in the reign of God on earth. Debate has raged over whether Luther's cross theology contains a sociopolitical as well as a theological vision. This chapter explores the interconnections between Luther's theology and the context in which it was lived, noting at the outset that Luther's theological vision prevents a thoroughgoing apolitical stance. Paul Althaus observes that, for Luther, "Concern for the true knowledge of God and concern for the right ethical attitude are not separate and distinct but ultimately one and the same. The theology of the cross and the theology of glory have implications for both."[1] In the years immediately following his presentation at Heidelberg, Luther attended to the real repercussions for daily existence—within both the church and the sociopolitical realm—of his cross-centered vision. The period from Heidelberg to the mid-1520s is hailed by many as the height of Luther's reforming genius, when his prophetic cries against ecclesial theologies of glory effectively brought down the walls of a corrupt church structure. But even while he risked his life to shout down the tyranny of Rome, he was still a sheltered monk who stubbornly resisted applying his theological vision of freedom to particular social, economic, and political tyrannies in the Germany of his time. How did Luther—the onetime champion of Christian freedom—become, as Peter Matheson puts it, "the hammer of the poor"?[2] While Luther believed his theology contained a vision of life concretely transformed by God's work on the cross, his prophetic insight in the ecclesial realm outstripped his ability to envision his theology's subversive potential to speak to the sociopolitical storms of his day. This chapter tracks Luther's very human struggle to preach, write, live, and act as a theologian of cross amid the crumbling walls of authority and order around him.

The Road to Reformation

The summer following the presentation in Heidelberg, Luther's heresy trial opened in Rome. Luther himself was summoned to Rome, but he appealed and moved the trial to the German city of Augsburg. In this same summer, Luther published his *Explanation of the Ninety-five Theses*, in which he continued his attack not only on indulgences but also on a host of common confessional practices that appeared to him to have no basis in Scripture. In these theses, Carl Folkemer observes, Luther "applied his newly developed theology of the cross . . . and challenged the authority of the church."[3] Even before he enlarged the claims embedded within the Ninety-five Theses, many already interpreted Luther's initial critique as a direct attack on papal authority. In the *Explanations,* Luther argued that indulgences promote a theology of glory that prizes ancient relics and monetary gain over the true relics of Christ's suffering and death. Luther dedicated the treatise to the pope, still believing at this point that "everything the pope does must be endured";[4] nevertheless, his cross-centered theology compelled him to rage against what, in his view, amounted to abuse of spiritual authority. That same authority summoned Luther to Augsburg to recant his views.

Traveling from his home in Wittenberg to the site of the trial in Augsburg, Luther faced his first serious encounter with real-life anguish on account of his new theological vision. Luther compared his situation to that of Christ, wondering if he would suffer and die at the hands of self-righteous authorities.[5] The stress of the journey left Luther unable to walk as he arrived in Augsburg. This striking scene offers insight into Luther's approach to suffering. For him, crosses are never chosen. Yet, remaining faithful to the gospel sometimes requires endurance of physical and spiritual suffering. Here again we see Luther's view of Christian suffering—including his own experience of it—as descriptive rather than prescriptive in character. Luther decidedly did not seek the perilous conditions of his repeated travels to defend his vision of Christian faith.

Standing before the cardinal in Augsburg, Luther was told to recant his statements questioning the pope's authority. The cardinal demanded that Luther publicly profess the final authority of the pope in all matters of doctrine. But Luther was committed to calling a thing what it is. He did not recant; still, he reluctantly agreed to remain silent on these matters with the understanding that his opponents would do the same.

Luther ceased preaching and publishing for a few months, but when his opponents continued to speak, he broke his silence, attracting new supporters and opponents to his cross-centered vision. In 1519 he was summoned to debate Johannes Eck, a masterful orator and professor staunchly opposed to Luther and emergent movements of reform. Eck began comparing Luther's ideas to those of Jan Hus, a forerunner to the Reformation who, a century earlier, had been denounced as a heretic and burned at the stake. But Luther welcomed the comparison, declaring much of Hus's theology "properly Christian." By publicly defending the words of a heretic, Luther effectively called into question the authority of the pope as well as the infallibility of church decrees. And with this defense Eck accused Luther himself of heresy. But once again the opponent's strategy backfired. Placing Luther squarely in the tradition of Hus, who since his death had become "a symbol of the Church where lay people stood tall, and Christ was all in all,"[6] only boosted Luther's popularity as a revolutionary fighting for the cause of the laborer, the farmer, and the peasant, all of whom were keenly aware of living under the tyranny of ecclesial—and, as we shall see, temporal—authority.

In academic and ecclesial circles, the debate with Eck heightened the acrimony between Luther's supporters and detractors. Humanists remained supportive of Luther and his criticisms of scholastic theology, applauding his focus on Scripture for theological argumentation. Detractors grew more anxious and angered as Luther's vision began to seep through the official religious channels and into the lives and hearts of peasants and princes alike.

Works Revisited

In his earliest years of lecturing, preaching, and defending his new theological vision, "the public had known Luther primarily as a critic of scholastic theology, indulgences, and the papacy. He was not yet a Reformer. . . . Thus it happened that Luther step by step applied his new insight to wider and wider areas, transforming it into concrete proposals and solutions."[7] Luther had already sketched the shape and contours of his vision of a cross theology, but as trials and accusations of heresy swirled about him, he realized his vision needed specifics. For example, opponents of his vision argued that his dogged emphasis on faith alone rendered mute any talk of good works. Luther began to write a sermon defending the status of good works in his vision, then expanded it into a "little book" on the subject. In the *Treatise on Good Works*, Luther vigorously defends the role of good works in Christian living, but repositions them as necessarily flowing from faith in Christ. Moreover, this treatise unmistakably shows Luther's commitment to the layperson over the ecclesial hierarchy. Luther argues that if theologians were truly concerned about the uneducated laypeople who fill the pews and pay for indulgences, they would preach and write in German, and Christianity "would have more benefit from this than by those heavy, weighty tomes."[8] Luther accuses the scholars and priests of teaching an improper relationship between faith and works. Instead of learning about faith, Luther claims, laypeople see the church lifting up the works of those "who have every appearance of being great saints" when actually they build "on sand their own works" rather than on faith given by God.[9] Any instructive discussion of good works, then, must begin with a clarification of faith.

Addressing the *Treatise on Good Works* to the prince, but writing it as if he were preaching to his own congregation, Luther explains how good works relate to faith in his cross-centered vision. He states that the first and most precious work is faith in Christ. The work of faith, however, cannot be mistaken for one work among others. It stands above all others, and only from faith can any truly good work follow. Luther critiques late-medieval Christendom's treatment of works, bound up with "building churches, beautifying them, making pilgrimages, and all those things . . . written in the ecclesiastical regulations." This operative view, Luther complains, has "misled and burdened the world."[10] Instead, Luther returns to his claim that when faith truly reaches into the heart, it transforms human existence. This transformation reorients not only one's heart, but one's actions as well. This means that living a life of faith no longer revolves around adherence to a set of regulations, as Luther intimates above. Rather, a faithful Christian "has no need of a teacher of good works, but . . . does whatever the occasion calls for."[11]

What does it mean to say that Christians need no teacher or guide in order to produce good works? We can see here the seeds of rejection of the monastic life, which Luther experienced as full of exhausting rules and regulations. Contesting such a life, Luther draws on the metaphor of marriage—an image easily embraced by the laity—to clarify the nature of a life of good works. If a husband and wife really love each other, "Who teaches them what they are to do or not to do, say or not to say, or what to think?"[12] It is simply the confidence in the relationship, in the love, that teaches and guides them in their actions. Pushing the metaphor even further, Luther insists that for spouses, "There is no distinction in works. [They do] the great and the important as gladly as the small and unimportant."[13] So it is with the Christian's relationship with God. The prism of faith provides its own guidance, and effectively levels any hierarchical ordering of works. Luther's honoring faith as the highest work, it becomes clear, ignites a revolution in the medieval vision of the role and effectiveness of good works.

A major motif of Luther's cross theology, the hidden presence of God, also reasserts itself in this reimagining of good works. In faith, Luther wrote, we understand that "God stands hidden among the sufferings which would separate us from him. . . . In suffering, God stands there ready to help in grace, and through the dim window of faith [God] permits himself to be seen."[14] The link between God's hiddenness and human suffering remains real for Luther. Here he reassures Christians that God has not given us a human body that we might "kill its natural life or work." Self-harm has no place in the practice of good works. The sufferings of which Luther speaks are primarily sufferings of conscience that can serve to kill the wantonness in our lives, but they also cannot be completely divorced from experiences of physical suffering. Luther insists that faith involves an acceptance that God—rather than human beings—is at work in our spiritual suffering to slay our sinfulness. This should be the Christian's focus, rather than any type of merit that suffering and affliction might be thought to afford us.

In Luther's vision, suffering clearly is not a work. It is not to be considered meritorious in terms of one's position *coram Deo*. Experiences of suffering should be interpreted by Christians as God-given trials intended first to shatter, then to strengthen faith. Luther's own afflicted conscience undeniably influenced his assertion that "the most dangerous trial of all is when there is no trial, when everything is all right and running smoothly. That is when [we] tend to forget God."[15] Does this mean Christians are to seek out trials? It was clear to Luther that in living out one's faith, suffering is inevitable. A theologian of the cross insists that operating in proximity to the cross means that trials continue to come, as does the need "to exercise and strengthen yourself in faith every day."[16]

Returning to the *Treatise on Good Works*, we see that the structure follows the outline of the Ten Commandments. Luther's lively interpretation offers deeper insight into the practical implications of his theological vision. The First Commandment—that you shall have no other gods before God—states the primacy of faith in God for Christian living. Without faith becoming the truth of the heart, Luther argues, you may call on God "outwardly with your lips," or worship God "with your knees and bodily gestures." But having faith means that your whole life is redirected toward "trusting [God] with your whole heart" and looking to God "for all good, grace, and favor,"[17] honoring God through the orientation of your inner life.

Luther's emphasis on honor deserves some attention, especially as it relates to his view of obedience both to God as the ultimate authority, and to earthly authorities that govern human living *coram hominibus*. While Luther believed that humanity lives simultaneously in both the spiritual and temporal realms, his primary concern was to describe human existence *coram Deo,* or before God. At this stage of life Luther was still a sheltered monk, preoccupied with the inward reality of being justified by God through grace. He was just beginning to understand that the second half of the equation—living a justified existence—required substantial fleshing out. But it is clear that for Luther, obedience to God *coram Deo* is bound up with obedience to "those in authority over us" *coram hominibus.* In his commentary, Luther unpacks the meaning behind the commandment "Honor your mother and father," insisting that for children as well as for citizens, honoring demands obedience. Children are to obey their parents as long as parents remain faithful to the commands of God. Luther acknowledges, however, that if parents stray from faithful adherence to God's commands, their children are no longer obliged to obey. Similarly, in terms of temporal authorities, Christians are bound to obey, unless their commands contradict God's. Then the requirement of obedience no longer applies.

This view confirms the primacy of the *coram Deo* realm for Luther: obedience to God takes priority over obedience to human commands. Yet clearly this monk, inexperienced with temporal affairs, wanted to convey a message in his treatise to the prince: he strongly supported social order. Luther claims that the power of the state (and other kinds of earthly authority) can harm the body but not the soul. Subsequently, the power of bodily harm is "a very small matter in the sight of God," and disobedience, while permitted in select cases, should not preoccupy the Christian's thoughts. When one is commanded to submit to a law that contradicts God, a theologian of the cross is compelled to disobey unjust authority and then accept the consequences.

The *Treatise on Good Works* bears witness to the correlation between Luther's expanded articulation of his cross-centered vision and the seeds of his gradual movement away from and out of the monastery. For Luther, the monastery eventually came to symbolize a religious place set apart from the temporal world, a place preoccupied with religious vows through which the spiritual elite would "bear the cross." But for Luther, the cross is never chosen. In the words of Rowan Williams:

> Both internally and externally it is encountered as a thing imposed; otherwise it becomes a human invention, a technique, a work. . . . Religious life negates the cross by institutionalizing it, controlling the range of possible demands that may be made. Paradoxically, what had been seen as the highest, the paradigmatic, vocation was regarded by Luther as intrinsically incapable of being a vocation at all.[18]

But before declaring Luther the deliverer of the death knell of the contemplative life, we do well to heed Williams's caution: "It is easy enough to show what a perversely mistaken valuation of monasticism is involved in the reformer's attack: but the moral and theological passion of the attack points to a deep malaise in the religious life of the time, sharply felt within as well as outside the cloister."[19] In many ways Luther embodied this malaise. But he envisioned Christians transcending it; he seized the gospel on his way out of the monastery and thrust it into the light of the public realm. In his renewed endorsement of good works Luther reminded hearers that the gospel calls on all Christians to serve God through their worldly vocations. In Luther's vision, the peasant living outside the village is given a vocation just as is the priest or the pope living deep within sacred walls. Although years would pass before Luther himself officially cast off his monastic robe, his new vision of Christianity helped launch an exodus from monasteries and abbeys.

Luther's growing body of sermons and treatises was for Rome like pouring salt onto an already gaping wound. In June of 1520, Pope Leo X issued Luther an ultimatum: either recant or be denounced as a heretic. With the tide of unrest rising to ever-greater heights, Luther once again stubbornly refused to recant. Yet again he went on the offensive. He was revising his initial stance of toleration toward Rome. Indeed, he was becoming convinced that the theology of glory operative in late-medieval Christendom effectively replaced Christ's primal office with that of the pope's, something Luther refused to tolerate. In the span of just five short months, Luther produced three treatises that unleashed a full-fledged reformation in sixteenth-century Europe.

Sounding the Trumpets

By the summer of 1520, the stakes were higher for Luther and his theological vision than ever before. He teetered on the brink of excommunication. The three treatises for which Luther is most famous—*Appeal to the Christian Nobility, The Babylonian Captivity of the Church,* and *The Freedom of a Christian*—abound in vivid scriptural images that invoke both the drama and the scale of the looming crisis. From the appeal to the nobility, in which Luther visualizes Rome as a Jericho walled off by a theology of glory that "will come tumbling down when the war trumpets are sounded, the clarion call for God's justice and truth," to the powerful vision of Christians living as an Israel captive to Babylon,[20] these provocative works aimed to call a spade a spade,[21] to expose what lurked beneath the gilded surfaces of the edifices of the spiritual elite. One need not read far into these scathing critiques of the "Romanists," as Luther called them, before concluding that Luther sealed his own fate with them. Indeed, he was officially excommunicated in 1521. "By such primal, powerful and overwhelmingly biblical images" Luther "found a purchase on people's minds and hearts,"[22] through the expansion and concretization of the theological vision he first presented in Heidelberg. The theology of the cross becomes a theology of reformation that shouts down the corrupt walls of Rome.

Authorities and Appearances

Central to Luther's theology of the cross is the necessity of seeing through that which appears attractive but ultimately deceives. Theologians of glory, Luther repeatedly insists, are caught up in what appears to be proper Christian faith, but in actuality they have dramatically misplaced their faith. Luther's "Reformation Treatises," as the three treatises mentioned above have come to be known, overflow with vivid examples of how the papists tip their hand and reveal themselves as consummate theologians of glory. They revel in their perceived power and the glorious works of their spiritual elite. Luther symbolically removes those robes of glory from the pope and the spiritual brotherhood, arguing in dialectical fashion that God's glory and promises remain hidden in what by worldly standards appear too lowly for God's presence. With his appeals to the princes and his cries of protest on behalf of the peasants, Luther demands the removal of the spectacles of glory in order to expose the authority where he insists it really lies: in the Word of God and in those whose lives have been transformed by the saving work of the cross.

In his *Appeal to the Christian Nobility*, Luther sidesteps the papacy, directing his remarks instead to the Christian nobility and the Holy Roman emperor, making the case that they are equipped with the power to march around the "Romanist fortress" and bring down those walls protecting the papal abuse of power. In the struggle for temporal power between the church and the state, Luther believed the papacy continually overstepped the bounds of its rightful realm of authority. Countering the conventional wisdom, Luther argues that the papacy could claim no jurisdiction over German nobility. The priests in Rome—just like any other Christians—must be subject to the sword.[23] Luther singles out the pope for attack, highlighting his operative stance as a glory theologian who has distanced himself as far as possible from the cross of Christ. The pope, Luther writes, "is not the vicar of Christ in heaven, but only of Christ as he walked on earth, working, preaching, suffering, and dying."[24] Just as Christ did not involve himself in temporal affairs, Luther argues, neither should the pope. But in their charade of calling evil good, "the devil becomes a saint."[25] Luther appeals to the princes to protect the German people "from these rapacious wolves in sheep's clothing" who "thieve and rob" by selling indulgences, letters of confession, and other tactics that fill their coffers and resulted in the "commodification of faith."[26] Just as Luther insisted at Heidelberg that glory theology always leaves one thirsting for more, so here he points to "the Holy See of Avarice" and its hunger for wealth. Such flagrant glory theology must be stopped, Luther cries; the walls must come down, and the German nobility must use its authority to instigate the march around the papal walls.

What, then, is Luther's role in bringing down the walls? By what authority does Luther sound the trumpet, or shout to shake down the fortress? Hearkening back to his views on obeying authorities in his *Treatise on Good Works*, we see Luther counseling obedience, *unless* to obey would require one to go against the Word of God. Luther repeatedly claims he is "duty bound" to speak out publicly against the theologians of glory. One of his targets is the claim, voiced repeatedly by his opponents, that only the pope can interpret Scripture.[27] Luther intentionally subverts that mandate throughout his treatises, claiming himself a fool after the apostle Paul in his proclamations of the cross of Christ.[28] Luther understood his authority to speak as flowing from the Word of God. And it is precisely because the Romanists stay clear of the cross of Christ, Luther intones, that they no longer possess true spiritual authority. He also believes that a cross theologian who denies the power of a church infested by the Antichrist would necessarily be rejected by those who hold inauthentic power. Nevertheless, a theologian of the cross remains confident that what is faithful is hidden under its opposite: "I know full well that if my cause is just, it must be condemned early on and justified only by Christ in heaven."[29] The glory theology of late-medieval Christendom, Luther believes, had long ago "lost Christ" in its sacraments, in its religious orders, and finally in the heart of its spiritual authority.

A central concern for Luther in the treatises involves the misrepresentation and misuse of the sacraments. At the heart of his reimagining of the authority and power of God's Word is his vision of baptism. As Matheson suggests, Luther reenvisions the church on the basis of baptism.[30] Luther accuses the Romanists of virtually destroying the authority of baptism, and therefore subverting the power of God's Word. All Christians, Luther proclaims, are baptized "with the same baptism, have the same faith and the same gospel."[31] Rather than highlighting the joy and freedom baptism brings the Christian through faith, says Luther, the Romanists have instead built walls of exclusive brotherhoods and orders, and made lists of vows that have come to function as a prison, enslaving the Christian rather than celebrating the freedom of a justified life. The theologians of glory, Luther continues, have constructed an elaborate path based on works that leads into a land where baptism, faith, and freedom are obscured. And where faith is rendered silent, Luther observes, "works and prescribing of works immediately crowd their place. By them we have been carried away out of our own land, as into a Babylonian captivity, and despoiled of all our precious possessions."[32]

In his first two Reformation Treatises, Luther faults himself for initially being deceived by the structures and decrees of the Romanists, declaring, "Now I know it's the Kingdom of Babylon."[33] Luther insists that Christians have been forcibly removed from the land where they understood faith as a gift from God, and are forced to live in a foreign land where the gospel is oppressed and the freedom of the Christian is held captive. Once again, "the glittering pomp" that appears to signal spiritual power and authority, Luther proclaims, actually signals the opposite. The authority question is flipped on its head in yet another, even more radical, way with Luther's vision of the "priesthood of all believers." Based on the radical equality among Christians in his vision, Luther was able to reimagine the relationship between laity and priest. Anyone who is baptized and given the gift of faith—even the most lowly and uneducated—belongs to the royal priesthood through the blood of Christ (Luther here relies on I Pet. 2:9 and Rev. 5:9-10). All the anointing, consecrating, and shaving of heads in the world cannot a Christian make. "The keys were not given to Peter alone but to the whole community."[34] In his *Treatise on Good Works*, Luther leveled the hierarchy of works, but here he goes a step further, leveling the status of all believers *coram Deo*. Contrary to the puffed-up claims of the papacy, Luther insists, Scripture testifies that no differences exist among Christians, for all are one body (I Cor. 12). The priest, then, differs from the laity only with regard to office. When it comes to matters of faith, all Christians "should have the power to judge what is right and wrong."[35] Not only are all Christians priests, but any and all Christians can be theologians of the cross, who then must protest the subverting of the gospel by theologians of glory—those preoccupied only with perpetuating an illusory vision of Christian faith.

This new vision of the priesthood of all believers has wide-ranging consequences not only for the relationship between priest and layperson, but also for church sacraments. With the walls crumbling around him after the publication of his *Appeal*, Luther goes further with the *Babylonian Captivity*. Here he "enters and takes [the church's] central stronghold and sanctuary—the sacramental system by which she accompanied and controlled her members from the cradle to the grave."[36] It is in many of the sacraments that Luther sees the Romanists' most obviously false pretense to power. If all are baptized into the priesthood, Luther proposes, talk of the sacrament of ordination becomes yet another "verbal fiction," created by Rome rather than rooted in Scripture. Luther also attacks the denial of the cup to laypersons (who are themselves priests, in his view), insisting that if the papacy read Scripture they would see Christ as offering "both kinds" to his followers. Talk of transubstantiation of the bread and wine also obscures the Word, and such reliance on Aristotelian categories amounts to nothing more than a "Babel of philosophy."

In another critique with vast implications for Christian practice, Luther proclaims that to call the Mass a sacrifice is idolatrous. There is constant temptation and opportunity to distance oneself from the cross and to embrace a glory theologian's view of Mass, and such glory theology, Luther believes, lies at the heart of the deceit of the Romanists. Mass is not a work accomplished by a priest; it is a promise that comes from God to us.[37] What kept the Babylonian-like captivity in place, Luther argues, is the assertion of the mediating role of the priest in the sacraments. "This not only disempowered the laity, it was perceived as victimizing them. . . . Instead of giving life, they had taken it away. The contrast with Christ giving his life-blood for the poor was obvious. . . . The spell of the enchanted universe was shattered, and the symbolic power of the priest challenged."[38] The purpose of *Babylonian Captivity* was to dismantle the tyrannical Babylonian rule. As a theologian of the cross, Luther calls a thing what it is, inciting Christians to "cast off the yoke of [Roman] tyranny," embrace their role as priests, and live in confident conformity to Christ's living, dying, and living again.

In Luther's vision, just as in Scripture, Babylon cannot be saved. What Luther trumpets is genuine reform, a release from Babylonian captivity. Yet Luther does not once suggest that he would abandon the church. Rather, he insists that Christians confess: "I believe in one holy Christian church" and not "I believe in the pope at Rome."[39] Neither the monasteries nor the trappings of Romanist worship were in and of themselves evil, said Luther. It was instead their value as works given them by the Roman hierarchy that was the devil in disguise. Luther dares to declare, "If [the pope] is not the Antichrist, then somebody tell me who is!"[40] The pope becomes depicted as the Antichrist because of the theology of glory that provides the backdrop for the sacraments and other spiritual practices. Confession, discipline, rendering holy the time of worship, all these have their place within Christianity. But the clarion call of reform is unmistakable; it cries for abandonment of the ecclesial status quo. With Luther's bold and tireless attacks on the glory theology of the church, he begins the march back to the land of Zion, back to the cross of Christ.

Matheson observes that for the Reformation in general and for Luther in particular, the gospel was not only preached, it was painted and sung. The Reformation was "more a song or a symphony than a system, more lyric than lecture, more a leap of the imagination" than a plan for social restructuring.[41] Luther presents his Reformation Treatises as a kind of music. "I know another little song about Rome and the Romanists," he teases his readers at the finale of his *Appeal to the Christian Nobility*. "If their ears are itching to hear it, I will sing that one to them, too—and pitch it in the highest key!"[42] Belting out the contagious tune that features Christ and drowns out the intonations of the papacy, Luther became the leader of a reformation that was bound and determined to lead the people back to Christ.

Christ for You and Me

In his treatises, Luther offered both critiques and constructive proposals for reform. The dialectic embedded within them springs from Luther's stance as a theologian of the cross, viewing Christian existence as shaped and defined by cross and resurrection. These three treatises add several verses to the song sung by a cross theologian about the atoning role of Christ. As numerous scholars have argued, Luther diverges in significant ways from traditional theories of atonement, which focus on an offering or payment back to God from humanity. This preoccupation with what human beings need to do to become acceptable to God was precisely the problem for Luther—for that is the focus of any and every version of glory theology. Those who find Luther's view of atonement distinctive point to what Gerhard Forde calls "a reversal of directions" that defines Luther's understanding of the cross of Christ.[43] A pattern of reversal can be seen throughout the treatises: Luther faults papal theology for projecting a vision character- istic of theologians of glory, professing the reverse of what actually is the case. When attacking the view of Mass as a sacrifice, for instance, Luther argues that "Christ's mass was most simple"; there were no vest- ments or elaborate robes. The papists' glorified view of Mass is mis- leading, Luther writes. Rather than a priest sacrificing *to* God, the reverse is actually the case: a promise come "from God to us."[44] Simi- larly, Luther accuses the papists of having reversed the true under- standing of baptism. This sacrament was "instituted to nourish faith," but "the pontiffs lead people as far as possible from baptism" toward a glory theology that burdens people with regulations and requirements, making them believe their salvation is somehow in the hands of those who set the regulations. Luther's reversal of directions restores the pri- macy of baptism and the faith through which one is justified by Christ's atoning work on the cross. Atonement, for Luther, involves what God does for us, not what we do for God.

Not surprisingly, Luther talks about atonement in dramatic biblical images and metaphors—such as the metaphor of marriage—rather than in abstract, theoretical terms. In his role as bridegroom, Christ takes on all of our sins, sufferings, and death through the "wedding ring of faith," and "acts as if they were his own and as if he himself had sinned."[45] This intimate, personal metaphor points once again to Luther's existential per- spective on the relationship between the sinful self and Christ, in which Christ takes on the sin as a spouse bears the beloved's burdens, becoming "a curse for us" (Gal. 3:13). Luther proclaims Christ as swallowing sin, conquering death, and redeeming his bride "from all her evil, and [adorning] her with all his goodness. Her sin cannot now destroy her."[46] Luther sees God as pursuing the only path possible to break through the sin and wrath that define human existence, through taking on, and ulti- mately dying with, human sin. But while this vision is central to a theol- ogy of the cross, the story does not end there. Luther's vision of salvation is a cross-to-resurrection reality: God on the cross defeats the power of sin and wrath on our behalf, giving us freedom to live a justi- fied existence in the light of Christ's resurrection.

This cross-and-resurrection reality is why Luther speaks of the "joyous exchange" between Christ and humanity. Christ takes all sin upon himself and bestows on sinners the gift of his righteousness in return. This joyous exchange is not a theory of atonement that demands intellectual assent. Rather, "our hearts must be captured by" the reality of this exchange of sin for righteousness.[47] The dramatic imagery of the atonement is vital to communicating its power for Luther, and such imagery should only enhance the conviction that "Christ ought to be preached to the end that faith in him may be established, that he may not only be Christ, but be Christ for you and me."[48]

The intimacy of the marriage metaphor punctuates the "for you and me" message of atonement Luther believed absent in the administration of the sacraments by the "Romanists." He complains that the Christ who suffered, died, and rose "for you and me" disappears behind metaphysical musings on the transubstantiation of the bread and wine. "Why do we not put aside such curiosity and cling simply to the words of Christ?" Luther cries.[49] If Christians quit listening to such a "Babel of philosophy," they could focus on the death and resurrection experience of faith.[50]

A theologian of the cross understands Christian existence as conforming not only to the cross of Christ but also to his resurrection. This reality is highlighted by Luther in his treatment of baptism. For the glory theologians of Rome, thought Luther, baptism is a symbolic gesture of the "death of sin and the life of grace."[51] Not so for Luther. For cross theologians, baptism is more than a spiritual or even a mental experience. "As soon as we begin to believe, we also begin to die to this world and to live to God as the life to come; so that faith is truly a death and a resurrection."[52] Because human sinfulness infects us to the core, nothing less than death will break sin's hold on us. This death, while not literal in terms of the heart ceasing to beat, is real nonetheless: in baptism, our sinful self dies and faith replaces selfish pride as the truth of the heart. In Luther's cross-centered vision, "Our whole life should be baptism,"[53] for through the cross we are forgiven, and new life becomes truly possible. Luther calls upon the story of Christ's encounter with the adulterous woman to dramatize the point. Christ says to the woman, "'Go, and do not sin again,' thereby laying upon her the cross. . . ."[54] If we could truly grasp the enormity of this gift,

Luther insists, "We would faint for joy."[55] The cross of Christ not only brings us low, as we heard so prominently at Heidelberg, but here the emphasis falls on the second half of the dialectic: it also releases persons from the captivity of works, rules, and regulations, to live in free and joyful response to God.

The Gift of Radical Freedom

Luther's dialectical understanding of atonement provides the foundation for his declaration of Christian freedom. This proclamation centers on how the cross sets Christians free to live a dramatically altered existence in the world. Exactly what Luther means by Christian freedom is embedded in yet another dialectic, which serves as the ground out of which his third Reformation Treatise, *On the Freedom of the Christian*, springs: "A Christian is a perfectly free lord of all, subject to none. A Christian is a perfectly dutiful servant of all, subject to all."[56] This paradoxical claim, and Luther's subsequent interpretation of it, contains for him "the whole of Christian life." First and foremost, we stand *coram Deo*, where our soul or "inner person" has been pronounced righteous through Christ's joyous exchange. Through faith we are set free to live for God. Luther impresses upon his readers that there is inestimable power in the fact that all Christians are "the freest of kings, priests forever." The believer is subject only to the Word of God, and the Word is "that which preaches Christ." This declaration of freedom, Luther insists, most certainly springs from the gospel message, for the gospel "teaches freedom in all matters."[57] In this light, Luther's refusal to recant becomes even more striking: the freedom preached in the gospel meant to him that Rome had no real jurisdiction over him. It could excommunicate him, but it could not rob him of his freedom to preach Christ.

But even as Christians bask in the glow of their newfound freedom before God, they also live *coram hominibus*. Christian freedom *coram Deo* does not alter one's necessary obedience to temporal authorities. But for Luther, however, Christians are to serve and be subject not just to rulers, but to *all* others. To experience the death of our outer, sinful self with Christ is to experience a shattering of all pretense. Living *coram hominibus*, where self-absorption has been broken, gives Christians what Otto Pesch calls a "freedom of conscience": Christians are freed to serve others without being forced to trust in the works themselves.[58] Being subject to all others, then, offers its own version of freedom—the freedom from keeping track of one's deeds toward others. Any scorekeeping ultimately coaxes one back to a theology of glory that encourages and fosters a preoccupation with self over others.

To prevent any glory theology from seeping into his vision of Christian freedom, Luther cautions against viewing subjection to all others as a new requirement demanded by Christ. On the contrary: when selfabsorption is broken and the Christian's gaze travels outward, conformity to Christ is experienced by becoming "Christs to one another and [in doing] to our neighbors as Christ does to us."[59] Through service to the neighbor, our outer, old person conforms to our inner, new person, through receptivity to the wounds and needs of those around us. This is how Luther defines authentic existence: "Here faith is truly active through love; that is, it finds expression in works of the freest service, cheerfully and lovingly done, with which a [person] willingly serves another without hope of reward."[60] Addressing again those who accused him of renouncing good works, Luther insists that in our capacity as servant *coram hominibus* we do all sorts of works. At times Luther's sharp distinctions between the inner and outer person may strike the reader as rather naive; yet Williams explains that

> it is one and the same reality which underlies the internal turning to God and the external serving of the world. There is one conversion; the Lutheran "conversion to the world" has little to do with the fashionable notion that God is to be found in the world or in the service of others rather than in prayer and interiority. If conversion does not begin in each person's private hell, in the meeting with God the crucifier and the crucified in the depths of the heart, there is no ground for the second level of conversion. . . . But once the self has been dethroned in the interior victory of God's righteousness, there is only one possible "translation" of this into bodily life, and that is the service of the neighbour. . . . The daily dying, daily taking of the cross, is precisely this exposure of the self to the devouring needs of others. It is "active holiness."[61]

Luther's "active holiness" never includes leisurely basking in the warmth of God's gift of righteousness and faith through the cross; rather, for Luther, discipline of the body is necessary so the outer person will "not revolt against faith and hinder the inner [person]."[62] Contrary to other statements Luther makes about the body's unrelatedness to the soul, here we see a more nuanced treatment of the interior/exterior relationship. Here the inner/outer dialectic is held together for Luther in dynamic tension. Outer practices affect internal character.

Because a life of faith is also always a sinful life, the life of faith must involve daily renewal. In free service to others, God "lets the cross take form" as we conform to the reality of the gift of righteousness given us by Christ. To freely embrace the cross of servanthood means that we empty ourselves of the daily temptation to become self-obsessed. Living in the flesh, Luther believes "we only begin to make some progress in that which shall be perfect in the future life."[63] Yet since we are only beginning, the cross remains our earthly reality. God's move from the cross to the resurrection already has been made, but—due to our own brokenness and the brokenness of the world—we continue our cruciform existence, understanding that "to preach Christ means to feed the soul, make it righteous, set it free and save it."[64] It is precisely from this freedom that hope springs: no matter what crosses we bear in this life, we hope in God's saving power to transform our earthly experiences of the cross into the everlasting reality of the resurrection.

With the publication of the three treatises in 1520, the gaping wound began to hemorrhage uncontrollably. Luther's opponents set his writings ablaze. Luther and his supporters publicly burned the papal bull. In the winter of 1521, Luther was summoned to the Diet of Worms, where again he was required to recant. His refusal at Worms continues to echo through the annals of religious thought. Luther declared, "I am bound by the scriptures I have quoted and my conscience is captive to the Word of God. I cannot and will not retract anything, since it is neither safe nor right to go against conscience." Then he added, "Here I stand. I can do no other. God help me! Amen."[65] On the heels of portraying true Christian faith as captive to Babylonian authorities, it becomes even more compelling to hear again the reversal of this theologian of the cross as he claims to be captive not to the spiritual authorities, but to the Word of God alone.

The faith given by God freed Luther to follow his conscience rather than the external commands he believed contradicted God's Word. Walther von Loewenich frames the significance of these words for religious history: "For the first time, the principle of freedom of conscience was exposed publicly before the highest ranking representative of the church and the world. One could make demands of everything else, but not of faith, for faith was a matter of conscience, [and conscience was] bound to God's Word."[66] For Luther, the transforming message of the gospel—that we are saved by faith—becomes so deeply engraved in one's being that conscience gains its place as a religiously authoritative source. This bold claim highlights the heroic significance of Luther's early career. As Matheson suggests, Luther's career began with "works of rare lyrical quality" that broke through the fortress and led the march back to faith.[67] Indeed, for most Christians of his day, Luther's vision of freedom was more aspiration than reality; yet it is difficult to overestimate the force with which these visions of freedom permeated the imaginations of the disenfranchised, the voiceless.[68] They were captured by the image of freedom, understanding its relevance to their lives in ways that would shock even the reformer himself.

For many, Luther's prophetic status only increased when the Diet of Worms succeeded in condemning and banning much of his work. It is also apparent that the authorities who put Luther on trial anticipated some fallout from his declaration of individual freedom of conscience in religious matters.[69] As we shall see, not everyone maintained the sharp distinction Luther maintained—or wanted to maintain—between the spiritual and temporal realms. Authorities rightly feared that Luther's ecclesiastical disobedience could easily spawn civil disobedience, unrest, and even outright rebellion throughout society.

A Political Theology of the Cross?

Fearing for his safety, Luther's allies hid him in a Wartburg castle immediately following the Diet of Worms. After constant public exposure and interaction with friends and foes alike, Luther fought against the silence and loneliness that confronted him in the castle. Back in Wittenberg, the spirit of reform was blowing in directions Luther himself had not anticipated. His vitriolic calls for ecclesiastical reform had fanned flames of unrest among Wittenberg students, professors, and parishioners.[70] Protesters destroyed icons, altars, and relics in area churches, prompting authorities to close city schools for fear that the violence would spread there. When Luther caught wind of the rioting and upheaval, he quickly abandoned the safety of his hideaway and returned to Wittenberg.

And what did this radical, irreverent, fearless attacker of the ecclesial status quo do to address the unrest? Upon arrival in Wittenberg, Luther immediately took to the pulpit, preaching for eight consecutive days on the urgent need for a less physically forceful approach toward reform. According to von Loewenich, Luther's pastoral inclination to preach likely prevented the Reformation from becoming an insurrection.[71] But unfortunately for Luther, the unrest extended far beyond his own congregation. Oberman places it in context, noting that "the roots of unrest had long been present in European history as a non-violent impulse for reform. . . . The new foment of the reformation proved to imply political radicalization by a biblical-spiritual opposition to the secular power of the church."[72] Luther, the monk and priest, was single-mindedly focused on exposing the papal abuses. While he acknowledged abuses by temporal authorities as well, he did not view them as impinging directly upon matters of salvation. But upon returning to Wittenberg, Luther quickly realized that a version of his reforming vision was beginning to catch fire throughout Germany. In response, he immediately penned a tract calling on Christians to refrain from insurrection and rebellion.[73] In it Luther reminded his followers of their status as "children of wrath," urging them to view current abuses by temporal authorities as God's punishment for human sinfulness. A strong state was needed, Luther agreed with Augustine, to restrain humanity's evil nature. The only type of insurrection Christians should even contemplate, said Luther, was "an insurrection of the mouth." Christ himself began such an insurrection against the glory theologians who filled his own day, Luther pointed out. Christians should then allow their mouths to become "mouths of Christ," and such witnessing to the Word would advance the cause of God's righteousness. But to understand how Luther's admonition to Christians to become "mouthpieces of God" interacts with the temporal realm, we must return to his concept of the two realms.

One Person, Two Realms

In 1523, Luther published *Temporal Authority: To What Extent It Should Be Obeyed*, in which he sets forth in detail his dialectical vision of the two realms (or "two kingdoms"). While this treatise stands as a significant first attempt at directing his attention toward societal issues, it is also important to acknowledge that Luther probably wrote it out of concern for "the excessive interference of the Catholic Church in secular affairs."[74] This pronouncement on political issues certainly was not Luther's last, and "was not intended to provide a definite theory of political obligation."[75] Instead, Luther addressed this treatise to a people steeped in an atmosphere of unrest, hoping to further expose the tyranny of Rome while simultaneously dissuading "overzealous measures by the population at large . . . [which] could succeed only in discrediting [Luther and those who followed him]."[76] Luther wanted to harness the momentum that existed for battering down the Romanist walls; but to do that, he was realizing, he needed to actively quell attempts to apply his vision for ecclesial reform directly to the simmering temporal context.

Before passing judgment on his vision of the dynamic between spiritual and temporal existence, we should take time to examine how Luther's vision functioned within his own context of a fracturing feudal society. He introduces the two realms with the insistence that God stands as ruler of both. Therefore, humans do not exist bodily within a profane realm, cut off from God. According to Luther, there is no sphere of life beyond God's purview.[77] God governs the earthly realm with the left hand, which, in the language of a theology of the cross, constitutes God's alien work. God's "left-handed governance," Luther insists, will never and should never lead to a theocracy, for true Christians always will remain in the minority within a given society. And while the gospel cannot rule a fallen society, "the fruits of the gospel break through to nourish the life of society."[78]

To talk of the gospel breaking into the temporal realm demonstrates the dialectical relationship between God's left hand of governance in temporal affairs and God's right hand of governance, under which people of faith are oriented toward the life and well-being of the neighbor.

While such dialectical thinking was customary for Luther, he acknowledged in the treatise that for many Christians, the existential reality of living simultaneously as a citizen of both realms is often accompanied by confusion. Even so, Luther argues that this paradox accurately reflects the existential life of the Christian: "the tension between creation, sin, reconciliation, and fulfillment" is a daily companion for anyone attempting to journey the life of faith.[79] Experiencing such a dialectic is the hallmark of life lived in proximity to the cross.

In *Temporal Authority* Luther offers guidance for Christian action in the temporal realm by calling attention to the limits of temporal authority. While princes possess authority to legislate behavior and actions, it is beyond their authority to legislate beliefs. Matters of faith belong to the spiritual realm, and as Luther proclaimed at Worms, they are ultimately matters of conscience. With this vision, then, Luther "allowed for the possibility of refusal to obey in cases when the prince trespassed upon the jurisdiction belonging only to God."[80] But before his followers could use his words as a rallying cry for social reform, Luther quickly invoked the biblical imperative of "turning the other cheek" when encountering abuse. Luther called for such physical restraint, Cynthia Grant Schoenberger suggests, not because he relished the vision of Christians suffering under temporal rule, but because he was concerned "with strengthening the state, the instrument he relied on for reform of the church, against the secular powers of the papacy."[81] This crucial point can get lost in assessments of Luther's vision of temporal existence, but its significance is paramount. We cannot get inside the mind of Luther, but we can appreciate the essential role princes played in his fight to shout down the fortress in Rome. Without temporal power on his side, Luther's words might have incited uprisings, but dramatic reform likely would have come much more slowly. Luther did caution princes against abusing their power, for he could already sense that people would rise up if the princes refused to restrain their use of authority. At the same time, however, he implored Christians to accept temporal abuses of power as inevitable; in a fallen world, God's proper work could only act under the guise of God's alien work. Peasants and other laypeople definitely could resist verbally, "through confession," but Luther viewed physical acts of resistance as threatening the stability of the social order, something he was determined to reject.

Yet Luther was convinced that being justified by faith *coram Deo* means that Christians are called upon "to live in the realm of the world . . . in such a way that the neighbor [is] always loved."[82] Since God governs both realms, Luther came to see that in the preaching of the Word, the minister is also called on to present a vision for faithful living within society. As William Lazareth observes, Luther's vision of the two realms combines religious receptivity with ethical activity in dialectical union, transcending the choice between social quietism and works-righteousness.[83] When writing on the topic of education, for example, Luther demonstrates this third way, stating that since the temporal realm will exist until the end of the age, "we need good, intelligent people to live in and run the cities."[84] Education of all boys *and girls*[85] contributes to a flourishing society. The freedom to be oriented toward the needs of the neighbor (and subsequently toward the needs of the neighborhood) opens up a plethora of possible actions by Christians in the earthly realm. While not eternal, the earthly realm still must be engaged by a theologian of the cross, for it stands under God's governance, and remains the place where Christians freely live out their response to God's mercy and forgiveness given through the cross.

Reform, Revolt, and Bearing the Cross

Despite Luther's efforts to preach reform and passive resistance around Germany, "the fundamental Reformation concepts, such as freedom and the priesthood of all believers, became slogans that electrified and mobilized peasants everywhere."[86] A group of peasants drafted and distributed a treatise of their own, recounting their grievances against the princes and announcing their platform for change. While Luther's defiant words and actions alone did not create the unrest that led to the uprising among peasants, it can be argued that Luther functioned as "a symbol, a beacon, a sign of the times" for the peasants,[87] and that his theological vision equipped them with a lens through which they could interpret and protest their experience of oppression. Although Luther repeatedly preached patience and endurance of the trials inflicted by unjust rulers, his noisy disobedience in response to papal injustices fueled the imaginations and religious zeal of the peasants set on ushering in the reign of God on earth.

In response to the peasant treatise demanding justice, as well as to the incitement of violence in parts of Germany, Luther published his *Admonition to Peace: A Reply to the Twelve Articles of the Peasants of Swabia*.[88] With this treatise, Luther attempts to cast himself as an impartial observer, admonishing both rulers and peasants for overstepping their given roles within society. Understanding his need for the princes' continued support, however, it is not surprising that Luther's words to the peasants carry much more force. "Do not resist evil," Luther counsels them. "The fact that the rulers are unjust and wicked does not excuse disorder and rebellion." He implores them to be Christlike, yielding and suffering any injustice thrust upon them by the authorities. Disruptive behavior, Luther declares, only demonstrates their unwillingness to suffer. He warns that if they actively resist, especially if they resort to violence, they "lay aside the claim Christian." In the face of temporal injustice, Christians can refuse—as Luther had done—to obey oppressive laws, but conformity to Christ's living and dying means relying on God for revolutionary action. Luther singles himself out as an exemplary theologian of the cross, one who refuses to obey and accepts the consequences. Because of his passive endurance, Luther reasons, his life thus far had been spared. He admonishes the peasants to follow his lead.

What exactly does Luther's *Admonition to Peace*—which looks more like an admonition to passive endurance of suffering on the part of the oppressed—tell us about the political implications of a theology of the cross? Is the cross theologian who flagrantly defies authority when protesting abuses in the spiritual realm relegated to patient suffering of abuses in the temporal realm? Jürgen Moltmann suggests that if we are searching for a political theology of the cross, we do well to look past Luther toward the left-wing reformer Thomas Müntzer. Even though he stood at the edges of the peasant revolt,[89] Müntzer and his theology deserve attention as we explore the intersections between a theology of the cross and the political realm. A contemporary of Luther, Müntzer was drawn to the apocalyptic sensibility of the Old Testament prophets, envisioning the kingdom of God as one day being realized on earth. In Müntzer's vision, as well as in the vision of many peasants, "the dignity of the Christian in baptism, so lyrically proclaimed by Luther, was given a communal twist. The Word of God freed the conscience but also liberated those in bondage."[90] This communalist vision led Müntzer and others to dismiss Luther's call for restraint. Christians had no time to waste, they protested: either they participated in the coming of God's rule to society—as the peasants were doing—or they became "godless" and would be destroyed by the current uprisings. For Müntzer, a theologian of the cross could not be content with an interior faith in Christ; such a perspective only fostered a false sense of security.[91] Instead, a cross-centered Christian must actively protest temporal injustices, taking up arms against those who threaten or work against the signs of Christ's imminent coming. This approach, Müntzer insisted, is the only option for a faithful follower of Christ.

Luther and Müntzer were two opposing interpreters of the political and social upheaval in sixteenth-century Germany. Yet both claimed to be faithful to the cross of Christ. Some have argued that the communalist vision rooted in freedom from serfdom may in fact have been the form in which the Reformation reached southern German villagers.[92] And while it sounds logical to contemporary ears that Luther's freedom songs were heard by the disenfranchised as a clarion call to political, economic, and social freedom, it remains unclear whether the peasants possessed a clear vision for a new world beyond the revolt. Apocalyptic scriptural references permeated their revolutionary vision, while life after the apocalypse garnered much less attention.[93] Luther viciously attacked Müntzer and the peasants who revolted, calling them patently unfaithful to Christ. To collapse the spiritual realm into the temporal, as Luther accused Müntzer of doing, could only be the work of a glory theologian unwilling to live as simultaneously free *and* sinful, necessarily obedient to external, temporal authorities. In late spring of 1525, Luther published an addendum to his *Admonition to Peace,* bearing the inflammatory title *Against the Robbing and Murdering Hordes of Peasants*. In this vituperative pamphlet, Luther positions himself squarely behind the princes, berating the peasants for stopping "at nothing short of revolution and overthrow of the existing social order."[94] While we can appreciate Luther's concern to support those authorities indispensable to his attempts at reforming the church, it becomes impossible to endorse the harsh, unforgiving tone he took with the peasants. Luther insists again that conformity to the crucified Christ is inconsistent with any talk of revolution or overthrow of existing social structures. Because the peasants committed violence in the name of Christ, Luther accuses them of "blaspheming God." The crucified Christ calls on Christians to suffer, Luther intones, and "a pious Christian ought to suffer a hundred deaths rather than consenting to the peasants' cause."[95] As punishment for the Peasants' War, Luther encourages the rulers to "take up the sword when necessary." He even goes so far as to admonish rulers to punish peasants without trial, in order to hasten an end to the ordeal. Although Luther penned this addendum at the height of the uprising, it was not published until after the rebellion had been crushed. Thenceforth the princes invoked it as support for their extreme brutality toward the peasants.

As many as one hundred thousand peasants lost their lives in the uprising.[96] Such breathtaking magnitude of Christian suffering did not seem to trouble Luther; he continually insisted that "God would save the truly innocent." We can only imagine the reactions of peasants who had hailed Luther as their spiritual inspiration: the man whom they regarded as the symbol of resistance had not only turned his back on them, but had also led the call for their demise. In the wake of continued atrocities by authorities in the revolt's aftermath, Luther's position came under severe attack by friends and foes alike. He finally yielded to pressure and published what was supposed to be a retraction. Unfortunately, in *An Open Letter on the Harsh Book against the Peasants*, Luther stubbornly stood firm in his unrepentance. He insisted that "anyone who knows how to distinguish rightly between the two kingdoms will not be offended by [the earlier tract]."[97] He refused to accept any responsibility for the behavior of the rulers, depicting their actions merely as proof of the reality of God's wrath. If Christians acknowledge the distinction between the two realms, he argued, they will understand the earthly realm as the realm of wrath, and the heavenly realm as the realm of mercy.

What are we to make of this Luther who becomes, in Matheson's words, "the hammer of the poor"? How compatible is his venomous attitude toward the peasants with his theology of the cross? Indeed, his cross-centered approach calls for a keen eye for any and all glory theologies that seek to place in human hands what rightfully belongs in God's. Had the peasants participating in armed revolt become theologians of glory? Even if that is the case, had Luther's descriptive approach to human suffering become a prescription for "suffering a hundred deaths" rather than working to improve living conditions for people of faith? Tackling this ugly chapter in Luther's career, Rowan Williams leads us back once more to Luther's conviction of the givenness of the cross "as the touchstone of Christian understanding." Luther expressed genuine shock at both the peasants' certainty of being privy to God's will, and at what he viewed as the pompous conviction that they themselves could usher God's reign into this broken and sinful world. In Luther's view, the peasants' positions amounted to "near-blasphemous trivializing of the terrible majesty of the Creator, the unendurable glory which has to be veiled in the flesh of Jesus crucified."[98] Luther's question to the peasants was "whether they have experienced spiritual distress and the divine birth, death, and hell; if they can produce no more than a catalogue of spiritual sensations, they are not to be heard. 'The sign of the Son of Man is then missing.'" In Williams's view, this constitutes "both the triumph of 'experiential' theology and the wreck of a mere theology of experience."[99] Their righteous certainty coupled with their determination to rid the peasant world of much of its suffering was tantamount, in Luther's mind, to abandoning the cross and the Christian life of being brought low by its judgment and wrath.

But is Luther's position on the Peasants' War faithful to his theology of the cross? Matheson helps set the stage for a response to this question, suggesting that "when a great shattering takes place and an enchanted world is lost, it can free us up to step out in new directions but can also toss us into the abyss. Dreams and nightmares frequently interweave. There is a nightmare dimension to the Reformation, too."[100] Indeed, Luther's stance against the peasants definitely qualifies as a nightmare. While the peasants may not have experienced the "sign of the Son of Man" in the way Luther envisioned, it appears that Luther himself underestimated the potential fruitfulness of the second half of his dialectic governing Christian existence.[101] In his treatise on the Babylonian captivity of Christians, Luther proclaimed that the bishop "has ceased being a bishop and has become a tyrant." We have appreciated Luther's concern for societal order, even if we lament the ways in which it prevented him from uttering the same stinging critique when it applied to temporal rulers. What is less appreciated, Matheson contends, is that Luther's central insight that salvation is by grace alone leaked into his "grace and favour" view of society, of prince and paterfamilias. The dreams of peasants that serfdom could be abolished, the hopes of artisans that they could participate in the running of their community . . . all these conflicted with his "grace and favour" perspective on society. He had toppled a hierarchical universe in the Church but still hoped to retain intact this layered universe and structures of the secular universe.[102]

As Matheson intimates, in this case, Luther's concern for preserving hierarchical distinctions seems a largely nontheological one, blinding him to the reality that "enemies of the gospel" can flourish in the temporal as well as the spiritual realm.[103]

Taking seriously the context in which Luther lived, Moltmann argues that the "church and society were too closely bound for the church to be reformed without consequences for society as well."[104] Luther himself repeatedly expressed concern for social reform, which followed quite naturally from his "recognition of divine vocation for every Christian" in the earthly realm.[105] A key insight of the Reformation, Moltmann suggests, is communicated through Luther's vision that the reformation of life necessarily follows from the reformation of faith. Despite his continued insistence that faith transforms the sinful self, altering the way the believer acts in the world, in the context of the Peasants' War this sheltered monk may have narrowed his cross-centered vision too far. To be sure, experiencing the "sign of the Son of Man" must remain an indelible component of any theology of the cross, and subsequently of humanity's sinful existence. Nevertheless, a cross theologian always identifies God's proper work, such as mercy, as hidden beneath the alien work of wrath. In condemning the peasants, Luther abandons any substantive discussion of God's proper work in light of the injustices they were forced to endure.

The gospel message of the cross had broken through Martin Luther's terrified conscience, and he fervently believed that Christ justified sinners like himself by making their sins his own. Luther's cross-centered vision allowed him to see most clearly the potential spiritual implications of the freedom God offers through the cross. This young monk's vision, however, remained blurred with respect to his theology's reformative possibilities for the peasants. I agree with those who claim that Luther's theological vision does not contain a political theory; nevertheless, with God as governor of both realms, a theologian of the cross must call a spade a spade in the temporal realm as well, particularly when religious justification is given for oppressive structures and practices. His single-mindedness prevented Luther from recognizing the crushing burdens that pervaded the lives of peasants who fervently embraced his vision of Christian freedom.

Freedom, Bondage, and the Will

Throughout the spring of 1525, Luther was occupied with the Peasants' War and its implications for his theological vision. His earlier focus on individual theologians of glory now shifted to social groups and factions. In the midst of this political upheaval, a onetime ally initiated a theological debate with Luther, compelling him to respond. Gifted humanist and biblical scholar Desiderius Erasmus issued a public challenge to Luther's idea of the unfree will. In his tract *On Free Will* Erasmus marshaled philosophical and scriptural support for the idea that humans can contribute to their own salvation through meritorious action.[106] Mining Luther's writings, he accused the reformer of negating human freedom by claiming that "everything happens by absolute necessity."[107] The stage was set for the debate, and Luther took up his role, penning *De servo arbitrio (On the Bondage of the Will),* in which he answers Erasmus's criticisms line by line.

While Luther later hailed his hyperbolic response to Erasmus as one of his best theological tracts, some scholars are more critical, considering the debate in its wider context. For example, Matheson calls their public quarrel "a nightmare to the countless thousands who regarded them as allies and passionately wanted them to continue as such."[108] During the infancy of the Reformation, the two had maintained an amicable relationship, even though Erasmus held more moderate views. When Luther began his march of protest, Erasmus declared support for his initial criticisms of the papacy. Subsequent events, however, caused Erasmus to rethink his position. According to Heiko Oberman, Erasmus viewed the

Reformation up to 1525 as a performance in three acts. It began as a humanistic campaign, in which Erasmus himself participated; then it shifted to a battle of words with Luther at its center, which he initially backed; but eventually it grew into an armed clash between princes and peasants, which Erasmus roundly condemned. For Erasmus, Oberman observes, this play chronicled the Reformation's spiritual descent into catastrophe.[109] And as Erasmus saw it, Luther's theology produced and orchestrated the nightmarish free fall into rebellion, disorder, and chaos.

More important for our purposes is what the debate can tell us about Luther's distinction between a theologian of the cross and a theologian of glory; Luther now placed Erasmus in the latter category. Erasmus consistently called for moderation, publicly avoiding the extreme edges of hot-button theological issues. At stake in Erasmus's quarrel with Luther was the choice between a more moderate, humanist anthropology regarding the will, and Luther's polemical Reformation view of human existence.[110] Erasmus wanted Luther to renounce the extremes and take an inclusive position, affirming the will as both free and unable to do anything apart from grace. For Luther, Erasmus's rational calls for moderation amounted to another theology of glory that admitted both human freedom and merit *coram Deo*—a move any theologian of the cross must deny.

Bound to Sin

Luther's response to Erasmus contains at least four elaborations on his cross-centered vision. To begin, Luther's methodological approach in this treatise reinforces those set forth in his theology of the cross. For instance, we quickly learn that Luther's objection to the phrase "free will" stems at least in part from his commitment to the reformation of theological language. Integral to Luther's approach is "plain, blunt speaking." Hearkening back to his accusation at Heidelberg that a theologian of glory calls a thing what it is not, Luther objects to Erasmus's description of free choice as a human rather than a divine affair.[111] According to Luther, Erasmus begins to speak the language of glory theologians when he depicts free choice as lodged in and springing forth from human will. In contrast, when a cross theologian speaks, human and divine will are carefully distinguished, as is the status of the human will *coram Deo* from its status *coram hominibus*. Since all freedom flows from God alone, the human will *coram Deo* remains permanently unfree. In divine matters—most importantly with respect to salvation—we remain completely dependent upon God. This affirmation must be reflected with the proper vocabulary, Luther believed. If the proper distinction between the two realms is made, then a cross theologian can agree with Erasmus that free choice is afforded humanity, but "only with respect to what is beneath [us] and not what is above [us]."[112] The absence of such a dialectic in Erasmus's work, Luther laments, leads to a glory theology that portrays human will as capable of accumulating merit that cooperates with grace and is applied toward one's salvation. Precise theological speaking must always acknowledge the paradox governing human existence, says Luther; otherwise the theologian embarks upon a journey of merit-seeking that leads to despair.

Second, and perhaps most substantively, Luther calls for proper theological punctuation on the depth and breadth of human sinfulness. Luther fears that Erasmus's stress on free choice and humanity's possible cooperation with God ultimately downplays the severity of sin—another serious misstep along the path trodden by glory theologians. In describing the extent to which human beings harbor sin, Luther shuns moderate speech. Because sin is rooted so deeply in our humanity, Luther writes, it leaves "free choice with no capacity to do anything but sin and be damned."[113] For Luther, no human will exists in a neutral state. Supporting these assertions with Scripture, Luther argues that in contrast to reason, the biblical text describes the human condition *coram Deo* as not only "bound, wretched, captive, sick and dead, but also as afflicted . . . with this misery of blindness, so that persons believe themselves to be free."[114] Theologians of the cross must allow the scales to fall from their eyes and see clearly the fallenness of human existence, our bondage to sin and to the clutches of Satan.

With his unwavering attention to sin, Luther attempts to remove all obstacles to faith and dependence upon God's grace to live freely in the world. Just as it was necessary at Heidelberg to tell how the sinful self is brought low, so in *On the Bondage of the Will* Luther again can affirm the "freedom of faith" *coram hominibus* only after negating the possibility of human freedom *coram Deo*. While Erasmus repeatedly emphasizes the cooperation between human will and God's grace, Luther repeatedly objects, insisting that only the liberated will can cooperate with God. Our will might remain unfree, but God acts through the will of the righteous, freeing them to a life of receptivity to any and all neighbors.

A vital dialectic Luther believed was missing from Erasmus's vision involves the distinction between God hidden and revealed—the third area of his cross-centered vision expanded upon in this treatise. Accusing Erasmus of relying more on philosophical categories than on Scripture, Luther insists that reason "makes no distinction between God preached and hidden."[115] This is a crucial error for Luther; without a dialectical understanding of God's activity, "reason demands that God should act according to human standards of justice."[116] For God to be God, and for humans to understand themselves as humans, we must accept that "the God we perceive in Christ . . . is only a small part of the majestic God who is above all things."[117] In other words, Luther acknowledges the reality of the God hidden beyond the revelation of Christ. For Luther, Erasmus's trust in the power of reason to view a fully revealed divine will leads him and other glory theologians to conclude that "a guarantee of truth and finality is bequeathed to a human group."[118] This glory theology threatens to create distinctions between human beings, while a cross-centered theologian preaches fundamental equality among sinful persons before God.

While Luther's talk of the hiddenness of God in this treatise echoes the prominent position of God's hiddenness in his theology of the cross, his discussion of God's hiddenness in *On the Bondage of the Will* may represent more of a contradiction than an expansion of his cross-centered vision. As Helmut Bandt admits, two dissimilar lines of thought become identifiable—one that depicts the hidden God *within* the revelation of Christ and the other that speaks of the God hidden *behind* the revelation—and they present a potential problem for Luther interpreters.[119] Some scholars try hard to reconcile the positions, but the innovative approach of Brian Gerrish, which allows for the sharp distinctiveness of both positions while simultaneously tracking their relatedness, gives a more careful account of the Luther texts.[120]

On the one hand, Luther is consistent with his theology of the cross when he speaks here of God hidden *within* the revelation of Christ. Like

Moses who was allowed to see only God's back, Christians encounter God's backside in the mystery of the cross, where God's strength, power, and presence are hidden *sub contrario* in Christ's suffering and dying. It is on the cross that God "hides" God's power by clothing it in the weakness of Christ's suffering humanity. On the other hand, in *On the Bondage of the Will* Luther also refers to a God hidden *behind* the revelation of Christ. This God cannot be glimpsed through the cross.

Why is this distinction important? For Luther, it is of central importance to know "whether the will does anything or nothing in matters pertaining to eternal salvation." He also wants Erasmus to understand that "this is the cardinal issue between us, on which everything else in this controversy turns."[121] How does the hiddenness of God relate to the central issue of salvation? In response to inquiries about the God hidden *behind* the revelation, Luther insists that God's will "should not be inquired into, but reverently adored. To the extent that God hides himself and wills to be unknown to us, it is no business of ours."[122] Gerrish understands Luther's admonition to refrain from inquiry as his pastoral response to the question of predestination. We simply cannot know why God saves some and not others. But, as Gerrish points out, this view not only is embarrassing for those who portray Luther as purely Christocentric, but also remains an unsatisfactory response regarding the relationship of loving God to the predestination quandary of why some and not others.

We must note that this unknowable, even menacing God behind the cross is not Luther's major focus in this treatise, yet "the predestining God remains in the shadows" of Luther's talk of God's hiddenness.[123] Pushing Luther on this other hiddenness fails to yield a logically satisfactory response. What it does lead to, Gerrish notes, is a reading between the lines as to why Luther refuses to probe more deeply into the predestination quandary. Gerrish suggests that it is impossible to read Luther and not recognize the terror of his own encounters with the hidden, presdestining God.[124] As Luther sees it, this hidden God is not only the predestining God, but also stands for the "'God' of everyday experience apart from Christ, what we encounter apart from the Word."[125] This is the God whose mask we cannot penetrate, the God of creation and destruction. But at the heart of Luther's cross-centered vision stands the claim that "we do have something to do with [God] insofar as he is clothed and set forth in his Word."[126] Through God clothed in the suffering and dying Christ, faith is given. Through Christ God has "lifted the corner of the veil," and what pulses from that mystery is the daily felt polarity of judgment and mercy, wrath and grace, death and life.

The God hidden *behind* Christ's revelation, in stark contrast, offers no comfort, and without the God hidden *within* the revelation of Christ, believers would remain in a permanent state of *Anfechtung*, something Luther was convinced could not be the case. Luther's expansion of his understanding of God's hiddenness, Gerrish helps us see, more clearly demonstrates why faith does not supersede the terror experienced in encountering God. As in the rest of Luther's thinking, the dialectic between the two kinds of hiddenness is woven into the fabric of Christian existence. Gerrish suggests that "faith takes on a kind of urgency because the hidden God prevents faith from becoming complacent."[127] Faith for Luther always presents itself as a kind of dare, a risk. It is defined not by placid reassurance that all has been accomplished by God; rather, it is defined by constant movement away from the God who remains unknowable toward the God hidden in the revelation of Christ's living, dying, and living again.

Luther's debate with Erasmus retains the sharply pointed edge reserved only for his battles with theologians of glory. For Luther in particular, much was at stake. When a theologian denies the hiddenness of God, denies the limits of human reason to decipher God's hidden will, and finally denies the terror that lurks in the region of any experience of faith, Luther believes the entire message of Christ's death on the cross is lost. And it is precisely the significance of Christ's cross and resurrection that stands as the fourth and final area in which *On the Bondage of the Will* expands on Luther's cross-centered vision. Luther faults Erasmus for an inadequate "emphasis on Christ," because, as Luther sees it, neither reason nor free choice reveals Christ.[128] According to Luther, Erasmus's preoccupation with free will dismisses Christ's essential role in Christian life. "If we believe Christ has redeemed [us] by his blood," Luther declares, "we are bound to confess that the whole [person] was lost; otherwise, we should make Christ superfluous. . . ."[129] Erasmus commits in Luther's eyes the classic Pelagian error, in which any affirmation of humanity's ability to contribute to salvation inevitably lessens the role of Christ. Luther was convinced that any conversation concerning free will must be rooted in Christ, for "the crucifixion of Christ gives us what we do not naturally have,"[130] the freedom to be oriented away from the self, toward the neighbor in love. In a cross-centered vision, only through Christ's death does God work in us, and as a result, the will is changed.[131] Christ's death, then, provides the condition for the possibility of Erasmus's claim to human freedom. But in the end, Luther accuses Erasmus of abandoning the meaning of Christ's death and resurrection. If the focus is on human merit, the cross is cast aside.

In opposition to Erasmus's mediating position aimed toward harmony, a combative Luther continued to answer "No!" to any attempt at taming his reformation message. To aim at moderation and harmony, Luther believed, would obscure or limit the power and freedom of God's Word. Luther envisioned the Word of God as bringing dissonance rather than a melodic harmony into the world. For Luther, Christian existence hangs suspended between two dialectically related realms. In *On the Bondage of the Will*, Luther depicts God's presence as disruptive. When God battles the forces of evil, Luther proclaims, "what can there be but tumult in the whole world?"[132] If humanity's bound will propels each person inward, and if the experience of God's alien work of breaking that inward focus is a daily one for the Christian, then tumult and *Anfechtung* are never far away. Whenever the gospel message becomes the truth of our hearts, whenever it becomes engraved within, it changes and renews the world from the inside out. Indeed, in Luther's vision, what else but tumult is possible in a world that rejected, tortured, and killed the one whose will was perfectly united with God's?

When faith and the experience of justification are engraved into our being, our lives are wholly reoriented. But "if we are under the god of this world, we are held captive to his will,"[133] and this radical reorientation meets with constant resistance. Theologies of glory constantly tempt the will to turn inward once again, to invest in some version of self-reliance, in which the self pretends to be in control but is ultimately captive to the god below. Luther accuses Erasmus of wanting to rid the theological landscape of any and all tumult. In Luther's vision, wishing away the tumult is tantamount to wishing away the transformative power of God as it works in and through the lives of people of faith.

✡ ✡ ✡ ✡ ✡

"If I didn't see the tumults, I should say that the Word of God was not in the world. The whole world is shaken and shattered on account of the Word of God."[134] The world of the 1520s in which Luther found himself was indeed shaken and shattered. The walls of the papacy were crumbling, monasteries were emptying, peasants were crawling out from under the rubble of their crushed rebellion. As Luther saw it, the power of the Word had been unleashed. The theology of the cross had survived battles and had become itself a theology of reform. But the birth of a new vision of Christianity came with a cost. Just after his prophetic cries of protest against the ecclesial abuses, Luther revealed a crucially weak link in his vision: that is, how a theology of the cross can be lived out within particular social, political, and economic contexts where abuse occurs. At best, Luther envisioned a dialectical existence for Christians that was coherent and indivisible. At worst, Luther shifted all his weight into the spiritual realm and refused to be receptive—as Christian freedom truly allows—to the wounds and needs of the downtrodden in the world. As we turn to the mature Luther, we see a theologian of the cross who remained committed to faith in the midst of *Anfechtung*, the God hidden *sub contrario*, and continued to attack any and all perceived theologians of glory who crossed his path.

3

Down to the Very Depths

We are beggars, it is true.
—Martin Luther

hen judging the significance of Martin Luther's life and actions, most persons are drawn to the youthful heroics of the Luther of Heidelberg, Wittenberg, and Worms. But what about the Luther beyond those early prophetic events? Does the Reformer's legacy benefit from the contributions of an aging Luther? In the older Luther, many argue, we find an ill-tempered, polemical, increasingly ailing man who defends rather than reforms the status quo. In his work on the later Luther, Mark Edwards maintains that this perspective—prevalent in modern Luther scholarship—"effectively diminishes both [Luther's] humanity and the context in which he wrote."[1] By the late 1520s the Reformation had become entangled with a myriad of social and political interests. According to Edwards, a fair assessment of Luther's later life must acknowledge the prominent role sociopolitical concerns played in his life and thought. This chapter seeks such an assessment.

But even as we probe the points of intersection between Luther's theology and the issues of his day, we maintain, as Gerhard Ebeling does, that a theology of the cross "serves as an indication of the object of his constant concern, the fundamental orientation of theological thought."[2] For Luther, a Christian's existence *coram Deo* was always before the crucified God. But as Luther himself admitted, there is a gap—sometimes wide, sometimes slight—between the gospel message of the cross and any theologian's attempt to live in faithful response to it. Let us turn to the later chapters of Luther's flawed attempt at living in proximity to the cross of Christ.

In addition to managing the Peasants' War and sparring with Erasmus, the early 1520s also presented Luther with the time-consuming, risky task of marrying off escaped nuns and priests. And although he argued repeatedly against compulsory celibacy for the seriously spiritual and for marriage as a "divinely noble" vocation,[3] Luther himself remained unwed. But in June 1525, Luther shocked friends and foes alike when he married Katherina von Bora, herself a runaway nun. Many criticized his timing; they married during the height of the Peasants' War. But Luther refused to back away from this controversy, just as he had with many others. Banned, excommunicated, and without a habit, this former monk took the last step in severing his ties to the Roman church by marrying. His marriage also represented the final shattering of the enchanted world of late-medieval Catholicism, which held that spiritual life forsook all things worldly. In stark contrast to the medieval imagination, marriage grounded the Reformer in the physical world, in the world of the flesh and sensuality. Perhaps, too, reversals came naturally to Luther, in that he chose to embody precisely the reverse of the late-medieval vision of a devoted spiritual life. The Reformation was reclaiming marriage, and although the effects were arguably mixed,[4] the radical nature of this defiant act remains.

His marriage to Katie and the birth of their six children immeasurably increased Luther's joys and sorrows. His writings about Katie, whom he said he grew to love "more dearly than myself,"[5] reveal deep affection and respect, and he also testifies that his children gave him joy and thankfulness. But amid this love and joy, the older Luther now practiced his theology in the face of sickness and death. He battled stomach ailments, witnessed the ever-expanding veil of the plague throughout his country, and endured the most agonizing of all sorrows for any parent, the tragic deaths of two of his children, baby Elizabeth and his beloved Magdalene.

"Lena's" death at age thirteen in particular filled Luther with inconsolable grief. He writes after her death: "The separation troubles me above measure. . . . It's strange to know that she is surely at peace and that she is well off there, very well off, and yet to grieve so much!"[6] Even while he remained confident that his precious daughter lived on with God, Luther could not shake the stinging pain of grief. And even as he came to embrace his own impending death, he continued to endured bouts of *Anfechtung* in the midst of proclaiming trust in God's saving grace.

While Luther's own vulnerabilities cast him as a sympathetic figure, we must acknowledge once again his own blind spots regarding the humanity of others. While Luther enjoyed many successes in his battle for reform, he also experienced many grim moments, realizing that true Christians were a rarity, and that most would remain mired in sin, despite the renewed preaching of the gospel.[7] As we attempt to understand Luther's later work, Peter Matheson suggests that "we may underestimate the grit it took to resist total despair"[8] in the face of the plodding and often compromised progress of reform. Against this background, we point to Luther's continued rants against his list of enemies of the gospel. Luther's vicious attacks on Jews and other perceived foes must stand alongside the genius of his reforming vision. Matheson comments on the language of Luther's tirades against his enemies: "When reality is gross, language becomes gross as well."[9] Luther was convinced that "one becomes a theologian through life"[10] through the messy, incomplete, and at times gross existence. At the same time he insists that theology must stand firm in the unchanging message of the gospel:

> It is quite evident that there is a great difference between teaching and life, just as there is a great difference between heaven and earth. Life may well be impure, sinful, and frail, but the teaching must be pure, holy, clear, and steadfast. Life may well be in error and not keep everything which the teaching commands, but the teaching (says Christ [Matt. 5:8]) must not lack one title or letter, whereas life may lack a whole word or line or the teaching. The reason is this: the teaching is God's Word and God's truth itself, while life includes our actions also.[11]

But to acknowledge the inevitable gap between the gospel teaching (understood most clearly through the cross, Luther believed) and human attempts to embody that teaching does not excuse Luther's tirades against others. When theology addresses the broken realities of human existence, it also commingles with politics, economics, and the social order. The task of a theologian of the cross, Luther envisioned in Heidelberg, is to bear witness to—rather than perfectly embody—the gift of righteousness offered by God's atoning work on the cross. But as Luther's life so vividly demonstrates, witnessing to the gospel is not a spectator sport. Luther fought tirelessly against any and all incarnations of glory theology that crossed his path. Nevertheless, the gap between theology professed and lived remains.

Christ Is Really Here

In bringing down the walls of the old sacramental system through his treatise on the captivity of the church, Luther hinted at a vision for the Lord's Supper that refused submission to the "Babel of philosophy" that held the power of the Word captive. As the Reformation grew in size and scope, Luther was drawn into debate with other reform-minded theologians (who came to be known as "evangelicals") over what this new vision for the Lord's Supper looks like. A detailed tracking of the eucharistic debate falls beyond our scope here. But in Luther's battle for the idea of Christ's presence within the bread and wine we can see not only his continued fixation on the encounter between the sinful self and the crucified Christ, but also the political fallout from disagreements among evangelicals at this critical juncture of the Reformation.

The latter half of the 1520s brought Luther into conflict with numerous "fanatics," his name for these most recent versions of glory theologians, over a faithful reformation view of the Lord's Supper. The most formidable fanatic Luther wrangled with over this vision was Swiss reformer and politician Huldrych Zwingli. Zwingli and others insisted that Christ's words "This is my body . . ." should be understood in a representative or symbolic rather than metaphysical way. The bread and wine never change into Christ's body or blood for people to ingest. The Christ of faith, Zwingli argues, sits "at the right hand of God" rather than in a piece of bread. Zwingli insists that faith is spiritual in character, and that Christ's divine rather than human nature is the object of faith. To Zwingli and his allies, the Lord's Supper constituted a "memorial meal" and Christian faith is oriented to the spiritual Christ above rather than in the enfleshed Christ below.

Zwingli's approach offended Luther's cross-centered vision, wherein a saving encounter with God comes only through God's indwelling in a human body that suffers and dies on a cross. Even though Zwingli's position represented an attempt to gain distance from the glory theology of the papists, Luther argued against Zwingli's glory claim that "Nothing spiritual can be present where there is anything material and physical." Actually, Luther insists, "The opposite is true. The Spirit cannot be with us *except in* the material and physical things such as Word, water, and Christ's body."[12] Luther admits that the concern to preserve the spiritual character of faith is the right one, but not through the separation of Christ's two natures. The spiritual character of faith for a cross theologian, Luther states, springs from the physical, embodied presence of God in the person of Jesus Christ. If spiritual comes to mean "heavenly" or "otherworldly," the humanity of Christ is severely diminished: Christ is taken "right out of the garden, [off] the cross, and [out of] the whole passion, saying that none of these things happened bodily."[13] We see at stake for Luther in this debate the intensely human, earthly reality of God being really here, with us and for us.

For Luther, Christ's presence in the elements of the Lord's Supper mirrors his conviction that the two natures of Christ must always be viewed as unified in one person.[14] Luther writes,

> You must say that the person (pointing to Christ) suffers, and dies. But this person is truly God, and therefore it is correct to say: the Son of God suffers. Although, so to speak, the one part (namely the divinity) doesn't suffer, nevertheless the person, who is God, suffers in the other part (namely, in the humanity).[15]

In the person of Christ, God's nature is so unified with human nature that the Christ's suffering now exists "in the Godhead itself."[16] At the heart of the Luther's cross theology lies the conviction that when God becomes one of us, God bears a mighty cost for entering into human flesh. And in turn, God's experience with physical, and existential suffering—embodied in the cry of forsakenness on the cross—is ultimately overcome, but never lost. Human suffering lives on in the very heart of God. While for Luther God ultimately transcends the earthly realities of joy and suffering, it is precisely here, in the beauty and brokenness of this world, that God meets us.

The vision of a unified Christ also influences Luther's interpretation of Christ's presence in the Lord's Supper. "Against all reason I hold that two diverse substances (bread and wine) may well be, in reality and name, one substance."[17] Luther continues, "We see how everything meshes together in sacramental reality." The Christ of the gospel is by no means bound to heaven or, in any literal way, to the right hand of God. Elaborating on his borrowed use of the scholastic notion of the ubiquity of Christ, Luther declares that "The right hand of God is not a specific place . . . but is the almighty power of God, which at one and the same time can be nowhere and yet must be everywhere."[18] In his effort to refute Zwingli, Luther argues that God cannot be contained by a piece of bread or by anything else in this world—but the incarnation confirms God's intimate presence with us, deep within our world.

What does it mean, then, for Luther to claim Christ's presence in the bread and the cup? Contrary to Zwingli, Luther claims that the words "This is my body . . ." witness to the real presence of Christ in the bread. When Zwingli suggests that "It is not glorious to be in the Lord's Supper" Luther hears the familiar drumbeat of a glory theology that lures people into a faith based on a speculative realm beyond this world. A theologian of the cross knows that because of sin, God's glory is hidden *sub contrario*, in places where glory theologians dare not venture: "The glory of our God is precisely that for our sakes he comes down to the very depths, into human flesh, into the bread, into our mouth, our heart, our bosom."[19] Neither a morsel of bread nor a sip of wine counts as a glorious location for God's presence, but Luther reminds those who tend to forget that neither is it glorious for God "to be born from a frail human body, or Christ to be led out to the wilderness, or be crucified."[20] God's power is clothed in the frailties of Christ's flesh, in the mundane reality of human existence. And in the Lord's Supper, which Luther called "an application of the passion" to the hearts of believers rather than the reenactment of it, God's presence comes to us. Here we see what Luther understood as the difference between his view and that of Zwingli. For Zwingli, no presence of Christ is to be found in the Supper other than his general spiritual presence in the church.[21] If an unbeliever partakes in the Supper, faith is absent and therefore so is Christ. In Luther's vision, however, Christ is really present, regardless of the spiritual condition of the participant. Through the partaking in the meal, the Word is externally present, and encounters the unbeliever initially as judgment. Luther speaks of the "alien faith," of the recipient who experiences the alien work of God. It is here, through the application of Christ's suffering and dying, that grace is given and true forgiveness is experienced.

But Zwingli was not convinced by Luther's appeals to Christ's real presence. He accused Luther of eating flesh, and of setting forth a vision of a "baked God." He even went as far as calling Luther a papist. Zwingli and Luther hurled insults back and forth, and this discord *among* evangelicals proved distressing for Philip of Hesse, political leader of Germany's evangelical region. Philip understood that a united evangelical front was critical to regional strength as well as to his own political clout with Charles V of the Holy Roman Empire. Given his personal investment in evangelical agreement, Philip brought the factions together at Marburg to broker a compromise. While in the end several points of agreement emerged, Luther and Zwingli continued to lock heads over the status of Christ's presence in the meal. With this failure to compromise, division within the Reformation was formalized. In the eyes of Zwingli and his allies, Luther remained a papist, holding on to a change in substance. For Luther's part, he stood stubbornly firm against the perceived theologians of glory for discounting Christ's objective presence within the meal. No final compromise was reached, which, as we shall see, had dramatic political consequences.

In assessing Luther's quarrel with Zwingli, Luther's opponents were justified in critiquing his view. For example, in opposing the interpretation of the Lord's Supper as a memorial meal, Luther failed to free himself from the substance metaphysics of his papal enemies.[22] While Luther never accomplished a successful defense of his doctrine of real presence, he nevertheless achieved several points worth noting. Once again, the rationality of a Zwingli or an Erasmus belies in Luther's mind the twofold reality of faith: the despair of the sinner is always linked to the joy of justified existence. For Luther, when the bread becomes mere memorial, the promise of forgiveness and true communion with Christ as both judge and justifier is in danger of being lost. This is why for Luther the Lord's Supper could not be celebrated enough; even though Christ's suffering occurred only once, the forgiveness of sins occurs "not just once, but as often as necessary." As it is with baptism, God is really *here*, in the water, in the bread. Heiko Oberman explains that for Luther,

> the infant in its nonage at the baptismal font and the dying man receiv-
> ing his last communion are not marginal figures in the Church of
> Christ. They stand for man at his weakest—whether at the beginning,
> the height of his powers, or the end of his strength. The idea that God
> is genuinely "there," outside the person, and can be found beyond the
> individual powers of thought and strength of faith is what the contro-
> versy of that time bestowed on posterity.[23]

While he fails to work out the details, Luther refused to let the key element of his vision die in this debate: the Word of God confronts sinners through the cross, first in judgment, then in love. In his debate with Zwingli, as it was with virtually everything he wrote, Luther's story is of Christ coming closer to humanity than most of his opponents could ever imagine. For Luther, faith is ultimately concerned with the heart being captured by the Word, by the external encounter with Christ, in the bread, in the heart.

Defense and Disobedience

As the Lord's Supper controversy illustrates, the religious climate in Europe suffered from deep divisions not only between Catholics and evangelicals, but also within evangelical movements themselves. In February 1530, Emperor Charles V convened the Diet of Augsburg in hopes of achieving a compromise among Germany's fracturing religious groups. Although the emperor set a conciliatory tone for the Diet, his allegiance was to Rome, which meant he was determined to proceed against the evangelicals "with fire and sword, should they not yield to his kindness."[24] At this point in time, the future of the Reformation still hung in the balance. Luther's theological vision "had not readily triumphed over resistance, as he had originally expected."[25] Even though Luther doubted that imperial support for the Reformation would emerge from the Diet, he regarded the movement's survival to be at stake in Augsburg. Luther understood the evangelical church to be embattled against the emperor, particularly in light of his threat of force should they refuse to compromise. To make matters worse from Luther's perspective, the imperial ban that had kept him from the 1521 Diet of Worms was still in force, requiring him to keep his distance from the actual proceedings. He remained in a nearby town throughout the Augsburg Diet, influencing the proceedings through frequent correspondence with his evangelical colleagues, most notably his close friend Philip Melanchthon, who emerged as the primary representative of the evangelical perspective.

During the Diet, Luther continued to adhere to his theology of the cross. The writings he produced throughout the proceedings embody the dialectic of critique and confession, emblematic of his critical yet confessional cross-centered stance. At Augsburg, just as at Worms and other diets and councils, the evangelical perspective itself was put on trial—and here we begin to understand what Robert Bertram calls the subversive character of Luther's confessing. Luther writes, "We appeared voluntarily at Augsburg, and offered humbly and eagerly to render an account. . . . [Not only that, we now] plead, implore, and clamor for a chance to do this, and suffer every indignity, mockery, contempt, and danger. . . ."[26] Bertram reminds us that humility in Luther should never be confused with modesty. Luther does indeed confess that "We have not attained all things or are perfect." Despite the sinful character of every evangelical, Luther believed they nevertheless "have the right rules" given them through the "pure teaching" of the gospel. Luther insists the Reformers submit humbly to the requirement to confess, regardless of the consequences. Light-years away from meek submission, Luther's humility carried a power that almost invariably led him to a public hearing.

Luther never shied away from submitting his theological vision to public scrutiny. Bertram notes the courage and tenacity required for such public confession, observing that "It is hard enough to be critical in a reformatory, prophetic sense of asserting criticism, but harder still to submit to criticism" while remaining true to one's initial confession.[27] That Luther was relegated to a supportive role at Augsburg frustrated him no end. He constantly encouraged Melanchthon to abandon his compromising tendencies and stand firm in confessing the evangelical position. Luther feared that his friend, in attempts to appease those whose opposition was backed by military force, would negotiate away the confession of Christ. In Luther's mind, the primary goal was to remain faithful to a cross-centered vision, and if that meant being charged with disobedience, so be it. While Melanchthon anguished over the possibility that failure to compromise at Augsburg would thwart his personal commitment to peace, Luther, in contrast, was concerned about the public confession of Christ crucified. On issues of justification, faith, and salvation, compromise meant for Luther that the gospel's proclamation was being prevented.

Because he could not directly control the outcome of the Diet, Luther resorted to penning a flurry of documents. He wrote to his colleagues negotiating in Augsburg, "Our cause stands secure. We know how we should believe and live, how we should teach and act, how we should suffer and pray, how we should recover and die [Rom. 8:28]."[28] The Augsburg Confession, presented on behalf of the evangelical cause, did not contain all that Luther had hoped. Nevertheless, when Luther heard that the Augsburg Confession was read at the Diet, he exclaimed, "I rejoice mightily that I have experienced this hour, when Christ is publicly proclaimed through this glorious confession by such men in such an assembly!"[29] For Luther believed that as long as public proclamation of Christ was possible, the Reformation would continue.

Despite the rigorous defense mounted by the evangelicals within and outside the proceedings, the edict of the Diet ruled against them. Evangelical regions within Germany rejected the edict under protest, and the Reformers at Augsburg refused to admit any error, further undermining the imperial authority and continuing to erode people's trust in their rulers. Amid such unrest, Luther and the evangelicals participating in the Diet were ordered to silently accept the edict. But true to his stance as a theologian of the cross, Luther actively rejected the commands both to remain silent and to halt the spread of ecclesial reform.[30] What appeared humble and submissive, then, actually served to further destabilize the declarations of those in power.

While Luther was embattled in defending the gospel on a national scale, his heart was never far from those laypersons filling the pews of the evangelical congregations. With the authorities at Augsburg ruling against the evangelicals' confession, Luther warned his "dear German people" that "I will convince you that it is God's command to disobey" the emperor's edict.[31] At this point the strategic potential of Luther's theological vision comes more acutely into focus. During the Peasants' War, Luther had called for the passive endurance of suffering by those who insisted the gospel was on their side. But now, says Bertram, Luther took an alternative—and ultimately more representative—approach toward suffering as an active, subversive disobedience.

> Whatever suffering befell the confessors they themselves had occasioned by what *they first refused to suffer*, the subversion of the gospel in high places. . . . Directly by the act of submitting their teaching, the confessors were nonetheless teaching, probably more publicly than ever and now in conscious defiance of ecclesiastical policy and, soon after, of imperial policy as well. . . . Whatever suffering the confessors were willing to endure was only consequent, rooted in this prior refusal to suffer. In refusing that, and in refusing to cease refusing, they were both ecclesiastically and civilly disobedient.[32]

Luther again envisioned human suffering as descriptive rather than prescriptive in character; faithfully following Christ must entail suffering. But as Bertram points out, all suffering is not equal. As Luther reminded the peasants during the uprising, much human suffering is the "sign of the Son of Man," the cross we bear for being human and participating in sinful existence. Perversion or denial of the gospel, on the other hand, must be met with resistance, and such resistance likely leads to suffering. This is Luther's unwavering conviction of the givenness of the cross. Christians do not seek out or create their own suffering, but when it comes to suffering on behalf of the gospel, it is taken on in faith.

In the aftermath of Augsburg, the disobedience of the Reformers stretched beyond the ecclesial into the civil realm. By 1529, the issue was no longer whether Christians like Luther should suffer martyrdom patiently. Rather, the question was a political one: Should Christian city-states and territories be expected to adopt the same martyrdom ethic?[33]

Returning to Politics

In the tense months following the Diet of Augsburg, Luther was forced to accept that the evangelical break with Rome, the emperor, and the Catholic regions was permanent. At the end of 1530, with encouragement from Philip of Hesse, Luther penned *Dr. Martin Luther's Warning to His Dear German People*, voicing support for the Protestant estates' cause. Luther was extremely reluctant to wade into the political waters of Protestant resistance. But he was faced with a painful choice: if he did not speak out publicly, his silence would appear as a tacit endorsement for the Catholic position.

Let us pause for a moment and survey the changes in Luther and the social, political, and religious landscape since the Peasants' War. In the early 1520s, Luther was a theologian of the cross focused squarely on the ecclesial realm, where theologians of glory came in the form of papists and their defenders. By the 1530s, however, the landscape had altered dramatically. Luther's reforming vision had gripped imaginations throughout Germany and beyond, but in territorial terms it had pitted evangelical regions against Catholic ones. The Reformation and its allies were threatened by the political will and might of the emperor. In this charged atmosphere, Luther concluded that his theology would have to adjust to the prevailing political reality. With the threat of force directed against his vision, his church, and his supporters, Luther realized he had little choice but to take a stand with clear civic consequences.

In his *Warning*, Luther addresses readers rather cautiously at first. He begins the treatise with the phrase "Assuming there is no God," as if to alert his readers that this theologian is wading into civil and legal waters. He quickly confesses that it weighs heavily on his conscience as a pastor, a "mouthpiece of God's Word," to "counsel war." But Luther immediately distinguishes his call for evangelicals to resist in the form of self-defense from the insurrectionist position held by peasant revolutionaries like Thomas Müntzer:

> He is an insurrectionist who refuses to submit to government and law, who attacks and fights against them, and attempts to overthrow them with a view of making himself ruler and establishing the law, as Müntzer did; that is the true definition of rebel. . . . In accordance with this definition, self-defense against the blood hounds cannot be rebellious.[34]

Luther is clear: he and the evangelical states were not trying to establish a new government. Rather, Luther is sanctioning armed protest against possible imperial takeover of the evangelical regions, which would lead to repression of their practices. This civil predicament required a civil response.

Moving through the treatise, however, we see that Luther's argument is more than merely civil or legal. He declares that not only are Germans permitted to resist the emperor, they are duty-bound to resist in defense of the gospel. Luther reminds his people that in baptism they "vowed to preserve Christ's gospel and not to persecute or oppose it."[35] If they did not resist the emperor, they "would also lend a hand in overthrowing and exterminating all the good which the dear gospel has again restored and established."[36] Luther and countless others had risked their lives for the Reformation, and he now reluctantly accepted that armed resistance may be necessary to preserve their gains.

Luther's cautious advocacy of armed defense of the gospel suggests a theological vision responding to its sociopolitical context. The atmosphere following the Diet of Augsburg, Luther believed, left him no choice. He could not be seen as serving the papist "Antichrist." Therefore, he found resistance the only viable option. According to Luther, Christ's gospel requires diligent defense, which always leads to the bearing of a cross—now potentially a physically violent cross—of one's own. Luther's consistent refusal to submit to ecclesial abuses finally overflowed to imperial abuses as well. When the gospel itself is at stake, the faithful, cross-centered stance becomes active resistance to any and all efforts to thwart its proclamation.

Promising Christ

In addition to dealing with the devastating effects of the plague sweeping into his world, the deaths of loved ones, and his own health problems, Luther spent his last years as a counselor to princes, in the role of "publicist in service to a religious movement."[37] In this role Luther penned a number of polemical tracts, some of which will be addressed at the end of this chapter. During this same period, however, Luther also produced one of the most significant accomplishments of his final years: his extensive *Lectures on Genesis,* written between 1536 and the end of his life in 1547. While the published editions of these lectures are based on notes taken by his students rather than on his own written texts, they nevertheless provide valuable insights into Luther's mature theological vision. As Martin Brecht observes, "[The lectures] reflect his participation in the developments, problems, and conflicts of the last decade of his life."[38] His theology continues to be intertwined with the issues of his day, and it is through these lectures that we gain further insight into Luther's continued articulation of his cross-centered vision.

But first let us consider Luther's approach to Scripture in general and to the Old Testament in particular. As noted in chapter 1, Luther abandoned the scholastic fourfold interpretation to Scripture early in his career. It was not that he disapproved of allegorical interpretation per se; after all, Luther admitted he met with fair success in his own attempts at allegory. Rather, Luther noted that creating allegories could tempt one to stray from normative faith claims.[39] Luther operated instead out of his law/gospel dialectic when interpreting Scripture. For Luther, the hermeneutical divide no longer stood between the Old and New Testaments, but rather in the hearing of God's Word through Scripture, first as a law of judgment, then as a word of salvation. With the collapse of the wall between the Old and New Testaments, Luther broke out of the medieval mind-set that pegged any talk of faith in Scripture exclusively to Christian or New Testament faith.[40] Abandoning the fourfold approach allowed Luther to declare early on that the Old Testament "fathers believed the same as we do. There is only one faith."[41] Their faith is in the promises of God, the same promises in which those who come after Christ trust. The promises of God in which all faithful persons trust lie within the claim found in Romans 4:25 that "without any doubt Christ died for our sins and rose again for our justification and life."[42] Luther understood the promises of Christ in threefold fashion: first, the promise of Christ's coming in the flesh; second, of Christ's coming within the soul of the hearer; and finally, of Christ's eschatological coming at the end of the age.[43]

Through his biblical exegesis of the Old Testament, Luther also rejects the medieval preoccupation with the imitation of Christ, focusing instead on the identification between Christians and the Old Testament faithful. The faithful, since the time of Adam and Eve, are seen as living under the same promises of Christ as do Christians. Likewise, the Old Testament faithful are all threatened and tempted to despair. These patriarchs and matriarchs stand not as moral exemplars for Luther; rather, their faith becomes a model for Christian faith.[44] Luther insists that "from the beginning of Genesis we have seen that two generations of human beings are being dealt with: the one of the righteous, which was the true church; the other of the unrighteous, which has always been the school of Satan."[45] Members of the true church cling to the promises of Christ, while the Old Testament witnesses to the false church through the characters who reject or ignore the promises of God.

Whenever Luther spoke of human beings, he was also always talking about God and about human beings *coram Deo*. Walther von Loewenich makes a similar claim when he asserts that "The theology of the cross— as it is presented in the *Heidelberg Disputation*—finds its development in the idea of the hidden God, and the concept of faith."[46] At this stage in his life, Luther was far removed from his presentation at Heidelberg. Nonetheless, that dialectic of God's hidden presence and the faith in things unseen remained a constant focus for Luther. Ebeling expresses a sentiment similar to that of von Loewenich, one that applies perhaps more readily to the mature Luther: "The concealment of God is paralleled by the structure of faith, which consists of concealment beneath a contrary."[47] Luther's theology of the cross, then, is also always a theology of faith. At the same time, we continue to be met with the painful reality that his theology is also inescapably a *"Theologie der Anfechtung."*[48] Throughout his lectures on Genesis, Luther remained preoccupied with the hidden God, faithful existence, and human beings as recipients both of God's "tests of faith" and of God's gift of salvation through the cross of Christ. Let us turn now to Luther's exploration of faith, God's hiddenness, and human beings' persistent battles with *Anfechtung.* The Genesis lectures attest to Luther's continued preoccupation with these issues, which lie at the heart of a theology of the cross.

Luther's Vision of the Old Testament Faithful

Commenting on the first chapters of Genesis, Luther acknowledges the likelihood of God's direct revelation to Adam and Eve before the fall. On this side of paradise, however, Luther declares that "This nature of ours has become so misshapen by sin, so depraved and utterly corrupted, that it cannot recognize God or comprehend his nature without a covering."[49] God is covered, clothed, in apparitions from the burning bush to the suffering experiences and death of Christ on the cross. Due to the prevailing reality of sin, people of faith are not emancipated from knowing God's proper work apart from God's strange work.[50] The law always accompanies the gospel.

In the Genesis lectures the notion of a God hidden *behind* the cross of Christ continues to find a place in Luther's theological vision. He still cautions his students to "avoid as much as possible any questions that carry us to the throne of the Supreme Majesty."[51] The proper domain of faith is what God reveals on the cross, where God "steps out of hiddennness into mystery."[52] Ian Siggins is right to claim that Luther maintains that God's will toward humanity is not unclear;[53] nevertheless, sin blurs vision, keeping God's work in the world shrouded in mystery and thus mysteriously felt, experienced, and understood. God's work and presence remain close yet ever mysterious since Adam and Eve turned their backs on God.

For Luther, God's presence and work took on this "backside" character when Adam and Eve turned away from God's gift of original righteousness, which resulted in humanity's becoming mired in the quicksand of sin. In keeping with a cross-centered focus on what is visible, Luther orients his biblical exegesis toward the actual sinful condition before us. Human beings no longer exist in their original state; currently we exist as mere "corpses" of the original nature. Luther claims that all God's sinful creatures are united through natural birth before God "in Adam"; the cross and resurrection initiate a new eon for humanity, one defined by forgiveness and renewal as sinners are baptized into the new age in Christ.[54] Luther's wrestling with the sinful character of humanity always begins at the cross. So it is for Luther that the affirmation of original sin begins with the cross and moves backwards to the stories of corruption. Revealed in the mystery of God's presence on the cross is God's wrath as a "truly alien work." Sin is exchanged for compassion and loses its ultimate grip on humanity. Divine compassion comes through a believer's encounter with the Word, Luther writes, through God's mysterious enveloping of human flesh, first in Christ, then "in us."[55] What is revealed through the cross is God's intention for humanity not to exist as corpses but rather as fully alive. Even while Luther resisted a vision of justification that spoke of a gradual process of healing throughout life, he retained the idea of healing in his exegesis.[56] With respect to the condition of original sin, Luther tells his students, "By Christ's death we have been set free. . . .This image of the new creature begins to be restored in the Gospel in this life, but it will not be finished in this life."[57] Faith, then, is what allows for the restoration of God's image within the sinner.

Luther continues his commentary by insisting that "Faith is an active, difficult, and powerful thing. If we want to consider what it really is, it is something that is done to us rather than something we do, for it changes and the heart and mind."[58] Mysteriously enveloping human life, God moves strangely to break the power of sin from the inside out, shifting our gaze away from stifling self-preoccupation outward toward the neighbor. Luther's encounter with Adam and Eve compels him to proclaim that humanity "was not created for leisure, but for work—even in paradise."[59] The work Christians are called to do, according to Luther, does not translate into a prescription for the monastic life. He counsels his students, "You should not be a monk. You should remain in the world and among people."[60] Luther views vocations as worldly "masks of God"; they are nothing other than the hands, channels, and means through which God accomplishes God's own will in the world. Luther thereby redefines Christian vocation, which, he insists, functions not as a means of salvation, but as the means in which God's creative work of love is carried forth in the world. As Mary Knutsen suggests, Luther's vision of Christian vocation "takes us not out but down into the depths of the world."[61] In living out our particular calling—whether as a parent, teacher, farmer, laborer, or prince—Luther insists that we experience the cross taking form where we are, oriented outward toward what Williams calls the "devouring needs of others."[62]

In his Genesis lectures, Luther heralds Abraham as the embodiment of a faithful living out of his vocation. Abraham predates Christ, but Luther marvels at how he wholly trusts in the promises of God, and "knew about [his son] Isaac that Christ would be born from him."[63] Luther notes Abraham's refusal to base his faith and trust in God on human insight or reason. God promises him a son, but decades pass before the promise comes to fruition. "Meanwhile Abraham, who is satisfied with the Word alone, believes the promise and simply clings to the invisible things."[64] Even in his steadfast faithfulness, Abraham reflects sinful humanity's inability to penetrate the majesty of God. Luther also reveres the unwavering faith of Abraham's wife, Sarah. Even through the trial of Hagar's bearing a son for Abraham, Sarah "does not abandon the faith or doubt the promise."[65] Rather than attempting to explain God's hidden and mysterious ways, Luther implores his students to follow Abraham and Sarah's lead: cling to the promises of God in the face of worldly appearances that utterly contradict them.

Luther's Abraham vividly portrays his dialectical understanding of the partial blindness of human existence. A person of faith accepts the unseen promises of God, trusting God's faithfulness. In the lives of the Old Testament faithful, Abraham preeminent among them, "We see a God . . . who comforts us, lifts us up into hope, and saves us."[66] When God speaks, Luther tells his students, we, like Abraham, "are to believe it and not debate it but rather take our intellect captive in the obedience of Christ."[67] This theme of obedience is consistently emphasized within Luther's cross-centered vision. When God commands Abraham to send away "his wife, Hagar," and their son, Ishmael, Abraham orders them away immediately. Luther notes that Abraham does not stop to question, debate, or challenge God. "Therefore," Luther concludes, "let no one add this detestable and fatal little word 'why' to God's commands. But when the command is certain, let us obey without argument and conclude that God is wiser than we are."[68] Trust in God's promise of salvation through the life, death, and resurrection of Christ gives the faithful assurance that "comfort follows affliction, hope follows despair, life follows death."[69] Abraham's unquestioning obedience reflects that this truth was written on his heart. Trust in the face of contradiction endures against all worldly evidence to the contrary.

Offering a potent illustration of an unfaithful stance, Luther turns to Hagar, who with her initial actions exemplifies for him "our pernicious and indescribable inborn disobedience."[70] Because Hagar bore Abraham an heir, Luther reasons, pride begins to seep into her heart, which culminates in her banishment to the desert. What most fascinates Luther in this story is the angel who appears to Hagar in the desert and commands her to return and submit to her mistress, Sarah. The angel's admonition, Luther declares, indicates God's respect for domestic hierarchy and order.[71] Indeed, Luther instructs the faithful to accept not only God's timing, but also one's given position in society. "No one should change position in life due to [one's] own judgment and desire."[72] Allowing oneself to be disciplined, Luther counsels, is what constitutes an obedient life pleasing to God. Obedient living is accepting one's calling, and in Hagar's case, submitting to the role of servant.

While Luther's critique of Hagar's disobedience may be a cautionary tale about selfish preoccupation, it is nevertheless another example of Luther's partial blindness with respect to what is divinely ordained. Luther labels unfaithful Hagar's refusal to obey what he considered "the orders of creation," that is, the "natural" way women stand under the rule of men, and slaves under the rule of masters, due to the ordering of creation after the fall. As with his views on the Peasants' War, Luther cannot see the potential societal implications of his cross-centered vision of Christian freedom. If he read Hagar's conversation with God in light of her eventual freedom glimpsed at the end of the narrative (Gen. 21:20–21), Luther's tidy juxtaposition of obedience and disobedience might have been disrupted and challenged. But again, the combined force of Luther's limited view of women, his alliance with societal authorities, and his preoccupation with human beings' spiritual relationship with God led Luther to an interpretation of the biblical text that supported unjust structural hierarchies even as he continued to attack those hierarchies within the ecclesial realm.

Enduring the Trials, Forgetting the Tears

Luther's exegesis illustrates his engagement with these characters, and his conviction that obedience does not come easily, even to the most faithful. What is striking to Luther about these stories is the intimate connection between obedience and experiences of *Anfechtung*. Although Abraham sends Hagar and Ishmael away at once, Luther observes, "Abraham did not do this without a very great struggle and very heavy sorrow."[73] Luther—as if himself a witness to this event—reports that Abraham obeys the command of God, all the while trembling in fear and anxiety at the heart-wrenching task. Such terror reaches feverish heights when God orders Abraham to kill his son. Luther comments, "Here God is clearly contradicting himself. Isaac is blessed, now Abraham is to kill him. There is a contradiction that is impossible for us to understand."[74] In the face of such blatant contradiction, Abraham, crippled with *Anfechtung*, "did not delay, he did not argue." Luther views Abraham as an ultimate exemplar of faith, noting that "I could not have been an onlooker, much less the performer and slayer."[75] Luther does not bring these stories to life in order to encourage taking up Abraham's cross. To the contrary: Luther insists that each person cannot and should not follow the same vocational path. Rather, Christians are called to follow Abraham's obedience, faith, and openness to the promises of God, even in the midst of the terrifying grip of *Anfechtung*.

Strikingly clear for Luther throughout the Genesis lectures is the undeniably dialectical character of a cross-centered existence. The Old Testament characters and events exemplify this powerfully: on the one hand, God promises Abraham a son. On the other, God appears to contradict the promise with a command to sacrifice this son. When contradiction occurs, Luther insists it is "merely a temptation" to cast doubt over God's faithfulness to humanity. Bypassing such temptation, Luther the pastor suggests, allows us to see the story as one that ultimately preaches comfort and encourages reliance upon the promises of God even when they appear in jeopardy. Old Testament stories like those of Abraham, Sarah, and Hagar reveal that theologians of the cross must confront the real experiences of trial and temptation that are endemic to sinful human existence. Trials are not only inescapable, but, Luther adds, they also represent the inevitable outcome of trusting in a God who often is hidden from view. "For under the curse, a blessing lies hidden; under the consciousness of sin, righteousness; under death, life; under affliction, comfort."[76] Experiencing life in constant tension between the two realms, von Loewenich explains, does not imply being confronted with absolute opposites, but involves "being addressed by the living God in a thoroughly concrete way."[77] Through these biblical characters Luther shows that living in the shadow of the cross does not mean sentimental adoration of a glorious God; it means experiencing life as recipients of God's judgment and love.

But what is Luther telling us about God here? He insists that it is through trials that God instructs persons "in a fatherly way," pushing us toward humility. As he did at Heidelberg, Luther tells his students about a God who "humbles his own, not because he wants to crush them, but in order that he may break down blasphemous presumption."[78] Luther points to Hagar as one whose pride in bearing Abraham's son needed to be broken. Through her trials in the desert, Luther believes, Hagar, "who was rebellious, becomes an entirely different person. . . . She is saying: now I see that the back which God showed me was his real face and that I am the object of his care."[79] Reflecting the dominant worldview of his time, Luther envisions little chance of changing one's given status; nevertheless, he encourages his people to be confident that no matter who, no matter what, you are the object of God's care. Through the devotional orientation of his writings, Luther captures the hearts of the German people.[80] Through Hagar's journey, Luther shows that faithful obedience—enduring one's own cross—transforms a person from the inside out. Hagar not only becomes a new person humbled by and before God, Luther testifies, but she also bears witness in Luther's eyes to how God's proper work—God's face—is revealed in and through God's wrathful, backside work of breaking down the self's obsession with itself.

Luther portrays Abraham, in contrast to Hagar, as consistently, faithfully humble. Why, then, does Abraham himself also experience the repeated terror of *Anfechtung*? Due to each person's persistent sinfulness, Luther states, trials also come to the faithful. The "tests" given to Abraham, Luther explains, are meant to strengthen his faith. The trials keep our attention focused on the need to rely on faith. Again, Luther speaks descriptively rather than prescriptively. He intends to embolden the faithful to face their own trials, taking comfort in the example of these Old Testament characters. For instance, even though God is behind Hagar's temporary banishment to the desert, when Hagar leaves Ishmael under a bush to die, Luther reassures us that "God hears the cries of Ishmael. This is a very great comfort for those who feel they have been cast out. . . . For [God] does not want to cast people aside. . . . And God cannot disregard the voices and groaning of the afflicted."[81] Convinced of the stories' pastoral significance, Luther says we may "conclude with certainty that God has regard for us, especially when he seems to have forgotten us, when we think we have been forsaken by him."[82] To the persons at the bottom of the social hierarchy, this message carries stunning power. When all is stripped away—as it was for many in Luther's day—these stories of resilience offer "very great comfort for those who feel cast out."[83]

But as much as Luther counsels against speculating about God's motives, he seems at times unable to resist the urge to offer explanations for the pressing, looming "Why?" that lurks within the trials and experiences of suffering. While Luther most often attributes it to God's wrath at work, breaking down sinful presumptions, he does, against his own better judgment, occasionally speculate more specifically: "God often causes even the innocent to experience the most serious misfortunes and punishments, merely in order to test them."[84] At another point he refers to God's temporary withdrawal from our lives as "a sport" for God. God "plays with" Abraham with the command to sacrifice his son. It is at these points where Luther comes face-to-face with that most unnerving reality: that there have always been—and likely will continue to be—innocent, faithful persons who nevertheless are beset with haunting, cruel, undeserved suffering. In Luther's vision, where God is always present and active, albeit in ways that exceed comprehension and rational explanation, there seems to be no alternative but to talk of God's alien work in relation to those who experience such life-negating suffering.

Amid the tension that lies within Luther's talk of God's involvement in human suffering and the apparent contradiction of God's own promises, Luther is consistent about one thing: his claim that God's wrath never outweighs God's compassion. "God sometimes allows us a breathing spell and assuages cares and misery with some comfort," Luther writes.[85] The theologian of the cross cannot avoid the reality of death. Luther's exegesis of Genesis is also replete with references to the apostle Paul, who speaks often of the existential and physical realities of death. "Paul often says, daily we die. Although we do not wish to call the life we live here a death, nevertheless it is surely nothing less than a continuous journey toward death. . . . Right from the womb we begin to die."[86]

Nevertheless, the lives of Abraham, Sarah, Hagar, and countless other Old Testament characters testify to the promise that God's wrath is penultimate, that death no longer has the last word. Tumultuous tribulations, though they often dominate life in this broken world, will not win the day. Luther testifies: "God doesn't love death, but life, just as in the beginning he also created man, not that he should die, but that he should live. Yet even after sin . . . God's will toward us cannot be unclear, that he loves life more than death."[87] For Luther, the cross of Christ is the interpretive lens through which reality is viewed. Any cross theology must speak first of wrath and judgment, then move to the gospel message of forgiveness and salvation. In Luther's eyes, nothing could more clearly indicate divine compassion than God's enveloping death and replacing it with the gift of life. God has entered human life, so much so that our suffering has been enveloped into the heart of God. Luther's vision of the God of the cross is a God who "takes an extraordinary delight in pouring forth compassion, like a mother who is caressing and petting her child in order that it may finally begin to forget its tears."[88] This image of a God who cares for her children with the fiercely tender love of a mother is one of Luther's most evocative images of God. This is the God hidden in the sufferings of the crucified Christ, the God who suffers with any and all who suffer.[89] This is the image he clings to, the one he invites others to embrace.

At the end of the day, Luther is much more concerned with what the trials mean for humanity than what they mean for God. His lectures are full of attempts to explain how trials are integral to a faithful life under the cross. As von Loewenich observes, for Luther "the meaning of the cross does not disclose itself in contemplative thought but only in suffering experience."[90] The Old Testament offers Luther, and us, ample evidence of that.

Crucifixions of the Enemy

While scholars agree that Luther's Genesis lectures restored a sense of historical significance to the Old Testament characters themselves—no longer were they merely "prefiguring Christ"—we nevertheless must face not only the dreams but also the nightmares that follow from Luther's exegesis, particularly as he speaks of God's continuing wrath against the unfaithful. Here and elsewhere, Luther portrays the Jews as the paragon of disobedience. Although Luther confessed that the chief doctrine of theology was "that God is the God of the Jews and the Gentiles, rich toward all," he quickly added that "because of their pride, the Jews lost their promise which was theirs and was due them."[91] Earlier in his life, Luther had adopted a more compassionate stance toward the Jews, admitting that if he had been treated in the manner in which Christians had treated the Jews, he too would have refused to embrace Christ as his savior. Luther hoped this approach would result in substantial conversions to Christianity. But when mass conversions failed to materialize, Luther went on the offensive, approaching Jews as enemies on a par with his other enemies, most notably the papacy. His final years reveal a Luther who had abandoned hope of converting those who opposed him. Instead, his writings were directed largely inward, intended more for the edification of his followers than for the remote possibility of transformation of his foes.[92]

Bertram notes that it remains difficult to assess the extent to which Luther's anti-Jewish views represent "merely a distillation and concentration of the traditional Christian enmity toward the Jews, and to what extent it was fed by special elements in his own theology or by the dynamics of his own personality."[93] Edwards cautions against linking Luther's statements regarding his enemies too closely or too quickly to his persona or his theology. He was a person of his day, for good and ill. In addition, his later years were often spent writing for commissions from political leaders. There certainly were moments when Luther was able to break out of his contextual perspective and envision a new imaginative world based on the bountiful grace of God. But more often than not, he was fully and sometimes dangerously a product of his time.

Edwards reminds us of Luther's confession that anger was his special sin. And it is just that anger which he unleashes on his enemies, most notably the Jews.

In Luther's stance toward the Jews, he begins where too many Christians have begun, with a claim about Jewish responsibility for the death of Christ. Luther insists that the Jews remain under God's wrath because "they killed Christ out of pure malice."[94] And because Luther viewed all Old Testament passages in light of how they preached the promises of Christ, he continuously found Jewish exegesis offensive to Christ. Bertram writes, "So clear is the christological meaning that [Luther] can attribute their nonacceptance of it only as willful blindness."[95] This does not mean that Jews are more sinful than Christians, however. Luther consistently emphasizes the common sinful nature of all human beings, Jews and Christians alike. Luther believes in a "solidarity of guilt" between Christians and Jews: "a common suffering under God's wrath, a common resistance to Christ, a common attempt to gain one's own righteousness and salvation apart from Christ, a common need for grace."[96] What differentiated the two groups, then, was their disposition toward God. A theologian of the cross exudes humility, a quality Luther judges as absent from Jewish expressions of faith. In this light, Luther reads the Old Testament stories as God's rejection of the Jews as the chosen people, arguing that "one dare not regard God as so cruel that he would punish his own people so long, so terribly, so unmercifully, and in addition keep silent, comforting them neither with words nor with deeds. . . . Who would have faith, hope, and love toward such a God?"[97] In Luther's rants against his enemies his anger at times overrides or even negates his commitment to a dialectical vision. In the case of the Jews, Luther aims to expose, time and again, how God *undialectically* opposes the Jews. Their hardships are neither trials of the righteous nor experiences of God's wrath wherein God's righteousness is hidden. Instead, the hardships represent to Luther the continuous experience of God's unmitigated wrath. Although Luther's cross-centered vision typically emphasizes the way in which sinful humanity sees God only in a veiled, hidden way, when it comes to the Jews, Luther's reading of Scripture leads him to conclude: "We see the facts before our eyes, and they do not deceive us."[98] God opposes the Jews; therefore, so should Christians.

Some scholars suggest that Luther's verbal assaults on the Jews are no more venomous than those he launched at his other enemies such as the papists. But for those of us reading Luther on this side of the long and painful legacy of violence done to Jews, what stands as even more grievous than his tirades is his blueprint for action. In his treatise *On the Jews and Their Lies* Luther instructs Christian rulers and laypersons alike to set fire to Jewish synagogues, destroy Jewish homes, and forbid Jews safe passage anywhere. These admonitions should haunt those of us living in the shadow of the Holocaust. When he calls to treat the Jews with "harsh mercy" he eerily foreshadows much modern oppression of the Jewish people.

Edwards insists that our assessments of Luther must consider his tracts on behalf of the civil authorities; in other words, his writings do not always reveal his true theological colors.[99] And yet prejudice against the Jews surfaces in Luther's writings as early as his first lectures on the Psalms.[100] Luther undeniably inherits and reproduces the anti-Jewish sentiments of his day. He was commissioned by the Count of Moravia to write a response to a treatise written by a Jew attacking a Christian exegesis of the Old Testament. After the first printing of *On the Jews and Their Lies*, however, a second printing was forbidden out of fear that the treatise could incite considerable violence.[101] In a climate hostile to Jews, Luther's calls for violence against them proved unsettling even to his own allies.

It may be impossible to determine the extent to which Luther's anti-Jewish convictions grew out of his theology rather than his cultural, social, political, and religious context. At the same time, this is a legacy that those who claim Luther must own. We must call attention to the inconsistencies in his claims that we (sinners) put Jesus on the cross— and yet Jews bear the responsibility for his death. We can also use Luther against himself, pushing his vision of the Old Testament as theologically significant in its own right to stretch to include Jewish interpretations of the text, as well as demanding a more nuanced dialectical approach to Israel and the Jews as integral to the Christian story. What we must say from our vantage point is that any contemporary version of Luther's cross-centered theology must work to sever the links that persist between Luther's cross-centered vision and an anti-Jewish bias.

✻ ✻ ✻ ✻ ✻

Facing what he knew to be the end of his life, Martin Luther uttered the claim "We are beggars, it is true." Beggars are all we have to proclaim the "pure gospel" teaching. Beggars are the theologians of the cross. This particular beggar, in brilliant yet deeply flawed ways, reimagined a religious universe through a theology of the cross—a theology that witnessed to the profoundly experiential journey of Christians as they are brought low by the cross, breaking from the suffocating grip of self-preoccupation and obsession. This existential vision gripped Luther from his earliest days to his last. But Luther's theology of the cross also voiced powerful calls for religious reform, shouting down the various theologies of glory that emerged from the religious landscape. Cross-centered theology expresses a twofold reality: it trumpets Christian freedom—which opens one up to a vocational calling that carries one down into the depths of a suffering, broken world.

Through his repulsive attacks on his enemies, Luther also descended to the depths of the world, and there, just as in his mightiest hour, he bore his own cross, the cross of judgment and condemnation. But Luther also believed that the cross ultimately gives beggars like him life in the midst of all evidence to the contrary. As we assess the legacy of this reformer, his accomplishments are undeniably paralleled by his blindness and his failure to consistently live out the compassionate existence that is the vocation of all who follow the crucified and risen Christ.

Indeed, these failures have led many contemporary theologians, particularly feminists, to reject his cross-centered theological vision. Feminists want to reject the Luther who hammers the poor, dismisses the role of physical suffering in human living, and denies the humanity of his opponents. But is there a way to retrieve Luther's theology of the cross in a way that avoids the blind spots? Part one has laid the groundwork for such a retrieval. We turn now in part two to feminist theology's relationship to Luther's cross-centered vision, and the possibility of crossing the divide.

Part
Two

4

Feminists Interrogate Luther

I am a theologian. I am also a woman.
—Valerie Saiving

n her 1960 essay "The Human Situation: A Feminine View,"
Valerie Saiving dared to occupy a previously invisible space on the
margins of Christian thought and practice. There she stood, calling
into question the theological tradition's persistent and often pernicious neglect of the space women inhabit when they dare to speak and
imagine theologically. The women who followed Saiving gradually gained
access to formal theological education and were simultaneously influenced by the North American women's movement of the 1960s and
1970s. They instigated a feminist movement of reform that has challenged Christianity to its core.[1] Saiving's imaginative leap represents a
contemporary move of defiance akin to Luther's "Here I stand" at Wittenberg. Saiving—and now many others—witness at once to bedrock
Christian affirmations that all persons are created in the image of God
and that neither male nor female exists in Christ, while also exposing
Christianity's deeply troubling record with respect to views on and treatment of women. The deep ambiguity lurking within Christian thought
and practice on the value and place of women comes from the history of
patriarchy: the social and church structures that consolidate power into

the hands of a few men, with others hierarchically ordered below them. As Christian feminism has grown, it has sharpened its analysis of oppressive forms of social organization to attend to the myriad of ways in which women (and men and children occupying those lower rungs of the hierarchical ladder) suffer under oppressive forces. Womanists, *mujeristas,* and women from throughout the two-thirds world all have challenged and intensified the focus on women burdened by these structures.[2] These voices make visible the reality that most women experience sexism in conjunction with other forms of oppression—racial, ethnic, economic, sexual, or religious. Christian feminism of the later half of the twentieth century initially involved mostly white, middle-class, highly educated women, and its proponents have had to rethink and revise claims regarding "women" and "women's experience" to honor this complex web of interlocking "isms" of which millions of women are a part. From the struggles of these diverse groups of women vibrant theologies have emerged: points of view from the underside that not only critique theology as usual, but also offer powerful visions of liberatory faith and practice, particularly to those who have been denied access to that theological space.

　　After decades of movement and growth, it is clear that feminists vary greatly in their visions for religious freedom and liberation. Nevertheless, this proliferation of feminist voices and visions has ignited a revolution within the Christian imagination, where the fullness of God's grace is witnessed to in the lives and concrete experiences of women. Feminist theologians stand in the strong and defiant tradition of Luther and other sixteenth-century reformers, laying claim to Luther's vision of *ecclesia semper reformanda:* the church as always reforming itself.

Feminist Reform and Revolt

Despite the increasingly multivalent character of feminist theological visions, a two-pronged typology developed in the 1970s by Carol Christ and Judith Plaskow continues to serve as a useful descriptor for feminist theological reflection today.[3] Christ and Plaskow distinguish between the revolutionary and the reformist streams of feminist theology. While both streams begin by critiquing oppressive layers of Christian tradition, they diverge with respect to where such critiques lead. Revolutionary feminists such as Mary Daly and Daphne Hampson argue that the oppressive nature of Christian tradition for women drives a permanent wedge between feminism and Christianity. Daly, mother of revolutionary feminist theology, insists that "If God is male then the male is God."[4] If women want to see themselves reflected in the divine and thereby treated respectfully within a religious tradition, so the argument goes, women must abandon Christianity. Hampson agrees with Daly, declaring that feminism "represents the death-knell of Christianity as a viable religious option [for women]."[5] According to Hampson, women operate out of an essentially different mode of thinking than men do. Feminism supports and affirms women's mode of thinking and is therefore diametrically opposed to Christian thought, which is viewed as advancing an exclusively male mode of thinking. The task of revolutionary feminists is to articulate a theology (or, more accurately, a "thealogy"[6]) that is woman-centered and unquestionably redemptive for women. Many feminists who embrace this revolution have (re)turned to the image of the goddess, the female deity who embodies and affirms female characteristics.[7]

While this book's orientation is decidedly more reformist than revolutionary, the revolutionaries are not to be ignored. As Sallie McFague instructs reformist feminists, "Few reformations would occur without revolutionaries: they are visionaries who imagine futures seldom if ever realized, but necessary for any decent present."[8] Reformist feminists share with revolutionaries a vision of religious redemption for women. The revolutionaries constantly challenge the reformers to never rest easy with any affirmation of the dominant theological vision. Here, the revolutionaries' weighty critiques of traditional anthropology and Christology will come into play as we struggle to give birth to a vision of a cross theology that is at once feminist and in the spirit of Luther.

While reformist feminists share in many revolutionary critiques, they also believe that the same tradition that has oppressed and excluded women is capable of proclaiming inclusive, liberating, salvific messages for them. Methodologically, reformist feminists often proceed along a threefold path of critique, retrieval, and reconstruction imagined as a continuing cycle rather than a tidy linear progression.[9] The first stage names the problem, acknowledging, analyzing, and delegitimating oppressive patterns within the tradition. Second, feminists seek out those counternarratives in Scripture and in the history of theology that speak against the dominant patriarchal stories. Reformist feminists believe that, while deeply ingrained, the narratives and structures that oppress are, in the end, not normative for biblical and theological texts. Finally, reformist feminists work to reconstruct "all the basic symbols of Christian faith to be equally inclusive of both women and men, and lean toward liberatory faith and practice."[10] This book follows a similar threefold approach, stressing that historical retrieval can include traditions that may have been introduced by men, but are suggestive of liberative possibilities for women as well.

Building upon traditions such as Luther's cross theology does not sit well with some Christian feminists, however. For example, feminist biblical scholar Elizabeth Schüssler Fiorenza argues that if feminists are going to approach the cross, they must "reconfigure it in a different frame of meaning . . . contextualizing feminist reflections on Jesus' suffering and cross within a different politics of meaning."[11] This is a serious challenge to those who attempt to reclaim a theological vision from a male theologian who resides close to, if not in, the heart of dominant Christian tradition. Despite the challenges, a growing number of women scholars are claiming a dialectical allegiance to both feminism and Luther's theological vision.[12] We embrace a reformist feminist perspective while simultaneously acknowledging the profound influence Luther's "grammar of faith" has on our own religious convictions.[13] Therefore, the politics of meaning of a feminist theology of the cross does not lead to utter rejection of Luther's politics of meaning, but instead aims at a mutual transformation of both Lutheran and feminist theological visions.

Still, feminist theologians argue that no doctrine is more problematic, and no symbol more potentially destructive to women and other marginalized persons, than the doctrine of Christology and the symbol of the cross. Exclusive focus on a male savior subjected to unjust suffering and violent death for the benefit of all human beings, feminists proclaim, all too often leads to harm for women.[14] For the vast majority of feminists, the maleness of Jesus alone presents a host of formidable issues, ranging from whether a male savior can save women to the perceived incongruity of picturing women in the image of Christ, and subsequently in the image of God.

In offering a feminist theological vision, this book must expose and keep at the fore the damaging history of effects from the cross of Christ over the centuries. Given its abusive history, many feminists have abandoned the cross as a theologically meaningful symbol. Indeed, use of the cross has become scandalous in ways the apostle Paul never envisioned: as supportive of oppression and destruction rather than of justification and salvation. Unfaithful uses of the cross force us to ask, along with Mary Boys, "In the face of the history that has disfigured the cross, should Christians lay it aside? Should they not repent of the violence it has justified and seek alternative symbols?"[15] While many feminists opt for or seek alternative symbols as more life-promoting than the cross, we cannot ignore the reality that the cross remains embedded within Christian imagination. At the same time, it must be said loudly and clearly that the cross cannot, should not, be reappropriated without repentance.

Moreover, I assert that Luther's theology of the cross is much more than a christological statement; it envelops the theologian within a vision of dynamic, transformed reality. When Luther and feminist theologians converse with one another, critique is not the only outcome. In their reforming sensibilities, they have some important commonalities that have not yet been sufficiently explored. In what ways do Luther and feminist theologians share a common vision?

Unlikely Allies

Until recently little had been written specifically on Luther and feminism. Initial conversations also remained understandably preoccupied with the first task of feminist theology, that is, the critique of Luther's theological vision.[16] But as more scholars explore the mutually enhancing conversations that might link these theological visions, method becomes an obvious point of connection. It can be argued that Luther shares with feminists a threefold methodological approach, including critique, retrieval, and reconceptualization. What follows is a sketch of several shared sensibilities that suggest the possibility of a feminist theology of the cross. These remarks are more suggestive than exhaustive; they begin to show ways in which the reforming sensibilities of these conversation partners converge, and set the stage for deeper, more substantive interaction.

To begin, both Luther and feminists utilize what feminists commonly call a "hermeneutics of suspicion," a process of interpretation that recognizes the provisional nature of interpretation and the tendency of interpreters to presuppose and enforce cultural norms and ideologies. According to feminists, Christian thought and practice overflow with particular theologies of glory—patriarchy, demonarchy,[17] kyriarchy[18]— that employ matrixes of domination in which women must live, move, and struggle to be. Feminist theology, in line with Luther's persistence in calling a thing what it is, calls the patriarchal assumptions underlying Christian claims by their real names. Just as Luther's theology of the cross puts everything to the test, including the dominant theological tradition he inherited, so feminists mirror this testing of tradition, scrutinizing its faithfulness to and respect for women.

Second, feminist theologians also employ a critical method that parallels Luther's constant warning of the seductive power of any and all versions of glory theology. That which attracts and seduces in a patriarchal milieu—such as what counts as acceptable images of womanhood—is often the same as that which oppresses and suppresses those on the margins. In response, feminist theologians set forth a theological vision from the underside of society, of history, an approach not unlike Luther's destabilizing move to the cross of Christ. Luther returns to Scripture, to Paul's cross-centered vision, retrieving this critical, subversive approach to counter scholasticism's seductively misleading claims. The God Christians come to know through the cross of Christ is the antithesis of the majestic God of the scholastics, who lives and reigns in power and glory. For Luther, God is met in the basest of places, hidden within suffering, pain, and death. In a similar vein, feminist theologians call attention to Christianity's forgotten and ignored elements—those that celebrate the power of women as agents and recipients of God's love. In a tradition that has more often than not denigrated women, feminists uncover and expose God's hidden presence in the most unpredictable of places: in the lives and experiences of women.

Third, Luther and feminist theologians both witness to theology's experiential dimensions. Both understand that people's beliefs must be considered in light of the challenges and struggles confronting them. For Luther, theology always stretched beyond mere intellectual exercise to faithful existence under the cross, requiring him to address the harsh realities of suffering and death. Similarly, feminists rely on the contextual category of experience to analyze and assess the practical implications of normative claims. Just as Luther determined that attention to the existential dimension of faith was missing from the prevailing theological imagination of his day, so feminists regard concrete experiences of women as missing from dominant theological discourse.

Where Luther and feminist theologians stand most closely together is in their reforming *sensibility*, exercised through the shared methodological commitments noted above. Both Luther and feminists are allied in their stinging critiques of dominant traditions. Both are well practiced in leveling a "No!" against the theologies of glory running rampant in each context. But indeed, this is no cozy compatibility; an important caveat must be addressed. In a recent assessment of feminist theology from the perspective of a narrative theologian,[19] Kathryn Greene-McCreight argues that feminist theologians consistently reverse the flow of theological interpretation. Rather than allowing the biblical narrative to "absorb the intra- and extratextual world" (the narrativist approach), feminists reverse the interpretive flow when they bring the extratextual locus of women's experience to confront and interrogate the biblical text. Due to this reversal, Greene-McCreight labels most feminist reconstruction "non-narrativist" and thus potentially fatally flawed in its task of clarifying Christian belief in terms feminists can understand and perhaps even appreciate.[20]

Greene-McCreight is right to believe that few feminists embrace a narrative approach to theology—an issue that bears more investigation in its own right. I also am sympathetic to her concern over the status of the biblical narrative: feminists at times succumb to the perennial pull toward a theology of glory that allows women's experience to become the final arbiter of theological claims. At the same time, however, we cannot ignore the fact that feminists accuse Luther of precisely the same sin: that is, of succumbing to the pull of glory theology when he uses his own experience of a terrified conscience as the basis for making universal claims about the human condition. The lively debate surrounding Luther's use of his own experience should lead us to be wary of Greene-McCreight's tidy either/or distinction between narrative and nonnarrative approaches. Are "narrativist" or "nonnarrativist" the only two options? For Luther, theology's relationship to experience was not a proposition in which *either* the theologian enters fully into the narrative world of the text *or* the theologian allows her experience to utterly determine her theological claims. Rather, the theologian builds his theology on a correlation between self and narrative, where experience makes a theologian, but where experience is always correlated to existence *coram Deo*.[21] Feminist projects, it can be argued, are also correlative in nature, committed to keeping self and narrative, subject and object, tightly bound. From a feminist perspective, the vast, textured work by feminists in scriptural and doctrinal interpretation and the documented "history of effects" of these patriarchal traditions creates resistance to embracing fully the narrativist claim that the text can or should absorb the extratextual world. Stepping out as a feminist theologian of the cross involves testing and stretching the elasticity of the narrative parameters of Luther's own cross-centered vision.

While I aim for a mutually critical, mutually enhancing conversation between Luther and feminist theologians, I note a persistent blind spot in both movements (although it is much more explicit and pernicious in Luther's): an anti-Jewish bias. Katharina von Kellenbach's study of anti-Judaism in feminist theology exposes the ramifications of claiming Jesus as the embodiment of a nonsexist, nonpatriarchal vision over against the patriarchy of Judaism.[22] Just as there are numerous versions of Christianity, so are there different versions of Judaism, and, as Kellenbach persuasively argues, feminists should pay more attention to Jesus's Jewish identity; otherwise feminist theology slips into another form of glory theology that speaks falsely about what is actually the case. Feminists concerned with using Luther must address this lacuna and work to rectify it.

When we allow the conversation between Luther and feminist theologians to move beyond shared methodological commitments, points of difference quickly emerge. Here, as we turn to the thorny issues of sin, suffering, Jesus's male identity, and the meaning of the cross, we will hear the feminist "No!" to critical aspects of Luther's theological vision; we will also imagine Luther's response to such criticisms. This conversation will pave the way for the emergence of a feminist theology of the cross.

Interrogating Sin

What does it mean to be a sinful human being? The initial feminist critiques of traditional understandings of human sin such as Luther's began by accusing male theologians of viewing sin through the lens of their own particular male experience, then naming that experience as definitive for the entire human condition. But feminists have argued that a woman's sin must be imagined in opposite terms from a man's: as a self turning outward, focused on others to the detriment of her own sense of self.[23] In her groundbreaking critique of sexist notions of sin (taking on Reinhold Niebuhr in particular), Valerie Saiving argues that the underdevelopment or negation of self is the sin of women, rather than pride or "will to power" of the Niebuhrian vision. The danger of this misdiagnosis for women, Saiving contends, is that if women understand sin as pride and subsequently embrace the "selflessness of love" as the cure, they wrongly will try to strangle any impulse in themselves toward a healthy sense of self-differentiation and self-concern. Saiving concludes that the "specifically feminine dilemma is, in fact, precisely the opposite of the masculine."[24] In order to call human sin what it really is, theologians must attend to the essentially divergent experiences of women and men.

While feminists remain indebted to Saiving's crucial insight, scholars such as Jewish feminist Judith Plaskow carry Saiving's analysis beyond its biologically based assertions about the differences between men and women.[25] Plaskow retains Saiving's central claim that women's sin is a failure of the self to turn toward itself. Rather than rooting this claim in biology, however, Plaskow develops a view of women's experience that focuses on the "interrelationship between cultural expectations and their internalizations."[26] Plaskow stays clear of references to sin as originating in the female self, opting instead for a sociocultural construction of women's sin that emphasizes how social factors such as race and class work in complex ways to construct female selves as generally distinct from male selves.

In her critique, Plaskow does not deny the legitimacy of the Lutheran "self turned in upon itself" as a description of human sinfulness. Rather, she sees the problem with this notion as its lack of awareness "of ways in which sin is a product of social experience."[27] When the social experiences of women are taken seriously, Plaskow explains, it becomes apparent that patriarchal social and cultural factors encourage women to live self-sacrificially. Many women, therefore, should not be concerned primarily with committing the sins of pride and selfishness. Instead, what feminists have labeled "women's sin"—that is, a self-sacrificial disposition—is actually held up as Christian virtue.[28] Similar to Saiving, Plaskow insists that if theology misdiagnoses women's sin, then theology will misprescribe its "cure."

Indeed, she questions whether the primary function of grace—the breaking of the inward-turned self—really applies to women. This "cure," Plaskow insists, proves "irrelevant or even destructive for the one suffering from the sin of self lack."[29] A more appropriate doctrine of grace for women would allow them opportunity to raise consciousness of "both the social context of sin and their own collusion with it," as well as the possibility of participating in personal and social transformations of such sinful contexts.[30] Put simply, Plaskow argues that sin originates in cultural and societal structures; therefore, the cure (grace) must be articulated in structural terms. Grace in women's lives must come through transformation of the deformed social and cultural structures that limit a woman's ability to develop her sense of self.

Drawing on the work of Saiving and Plaskow, Daphne Hampson takes on Luther's understanding of sin and the human condition directly. She begins by acknowledging what she considers Luther's achievement: his reconceptualization of the human being's relationship to God. Luther explained that persons of faith live not in themselves, but rather with their sense of self grounded outside themselves, in God. Since humanity "naturally" tends to turn in upon itself, Hampson notes, Luther's understanding of faithful existence ultimately requires an "unnatural" trust in the conviction that who we are must lie with another, namely, God. Luther's all-consuming focus on *coram Deo* existence, Hampson asserts, results in a self that can be secure only within faithful relationship to God. Luther's notion of self remains insecure with respect to relationships with other persons and, subsequently, out of place in the world in general.

Hampson's critiques echo those of Saiving and Plaskow when she expresses doubt that women experience anything like the sense of anxiety stemming from the isolation of the self from God, as vividly communicated in Luther's talk of *Anfechtung*. According to Hampson, women possess an "essential connectedness with others, a relationality that is integral to the self."[31] Therefore, Hampson follows Plaskow's lead in protesting Luther's call for the "self to be broken," noting its irrelevance and counterproductivity for women. Although Luther's analysis "tends to fit men," if men could develop a relationality akin to what women "naturally have," a violent breaking of the self would become unnecessary.[32] But while women are inherently relational, it appears that men are not inherently isolated and full of pride. Diverging from Saiving, Hampson implies that men also possess the inherent potential to be relational—but unhealthy patriarchal structures create obstacles to healthy relationships. Hampson concludes that Luther's diagnosis of sin currently applies to men, but not to women.

Although women often experience an "emptiness" or a "lack of centeredness" in a patriarchal society,[33] relationality nevertheless takes on salvific proportions for Hampson. While Luther depended upon God to transform his personal and social existence, Hampson insists women can experience such a transformation through relationships with other persons. And because feminism can help women (and men) actualize their potential for right relations with others, Hampson believes feminists have no need for Christianity, particularly in its Lutheran form.[34] They can transform oppressive structures and achieve salvation on their own through right relationship with others.

Building one upon the other, these critiques culminate in the conclusion—framed recently by Serene Jones—that Luther's sin-talk leaves no place for a woman's specificity as "woman."[35] In other words, Luther's analysis of sin misses the mark when tested against the experiences of women. Yet Jones is careful not to rule out entirely the possibility that Luther's analysis could fit women. She writes that woman "will fit the role [of Luther's 'sinner'] only insofar as she identifies herself as part of Luther's masculine subject."[36] While the debate continues over whether gender differences are innate or sociocultural, on either ground, feminist theologians call into question Luther's depiction of human sinfulness. The question becomes, then, does Luther universalize his particular (male) experience and claim its validity for all? And, relatedly, can women find themselves in Luther's story only by admitting to masculine patterns of existence?

Feminists and Luther in Dialogue

As we move into a dialogue between feminist theologians and Luther, we begin with one Lutheran woman's contestation of the aforementioned feminist visions. Rebecca Frey offers an alternative to this feminist challenge of traditional notions of sin, claiming that pride does represent an appropriate diagnosis of women's sin. Women in American society, Frey proposes, learn and reproduce forms of spiritual pride. Rather than suffering from a "defective sense of self," women learn to glorify a different set of behaviors than men. Instead of magnifying one's own "power, righteousness, and knowledge"—Niebuhr's description of the manifestations of pride—women boast of their sacrifices to others.

Frey points out that Luther considered lack of faith—or disbelief—one of humanity's gravest sins. The sin of disbelief occurs when we place trust in ourselves and our own abilities, eclipsing God. For Luther, disbelief is the primary manifestation of pride. What Frey suggests is that women are guilty of this same sin. "God gets lost in the shuffle as one busies oneself with other human beings," she writes.[37] Losing God amid the details of life results in the transference of faith and trust in God to faith and trust in oneself. Although Frey agrees that the sins of women and men deserve some separate attention and analysis, she challenges the notion that if the experiences of women are taken seriously, sin's diagnosis must undergo substantial alteration. Societal structures undeniably shape women's expressions of pride, but the origin of the sin of women runs deeper than societal structures, she contends. Women's sin is embedded in the individual herself, which results in a reaffirmation of original sin.[38]

While Frey's position remains within the confines of a gender essentialism that suggests women qua women experience a shared reality of pride in self-giving, she nevertheless offers a view of Luther's formulation of sin that includes not just masculine but feminine patterns of behavior. The vision of sin as the inward-turned self or as unbelief, which Otto Pesch describes as "a distorted picture of what we are called to be,"[39] is useful for a feminist cross-centered vision of sin.

But feminists like Hampson find an embrace of Luther's understanding of sin problematic, arguing that Luther's preoccupation with anxiety stemmed from self-isolation. As we imagine Luther in conversation with Hampson, we must ask, do these criticisms accurately reflect Luther's own struggle? Again we return to Luther's experiences of *Anfechtung*, the terror of God's absence through what he referred to as trials and temptations. Eric Gritsch suggests that for Luther, "theology [was] always governed by real, specific struggles in life, the real 'temptation' (*Anfechtung*)."[40] Because the gift of faith does not eliminate the presence of sin, Luther declared, these trials and temptations persist throughout life.

Luther's *Anfechtung* was more than anything an affliction of conscience. Clearly, the lives of women are not without trials. One need not read far into the therapeutic literature on women to be staggered by the prevalence of depression, anxiety, and eating disorders that plague contemporary women. In addition, for the vast majority of Western history, women have been deemed regulators and sustainers of the private, domestic (that is, relational) sphere of society.[41] Women have been regarded as responsible for equipping their children with the tools for creating right relationships. Feminists like Hampson assert that women have the power to overcome the trials that lurk within relationships, that they can broker peace between feuding parties, and that they can model right ways of relating to others. Hampson rallies for women to "claim power" in society, and then model for the public arena "a different way of interacting"—one that will transform patriarchal social structures.

Feminists rightly claim that women are experienced with these relational issues. Feminist theologians are also correct when they assert that social institutions with (hetero)sexist histories—such as marriage—could benefit from looking to women's relationships as models for human interaction.[42] Women and women's groups offer and enact healing, healthy relationships. Yet, if we are not careful, assertions like these can contribute to a theology of glory that mistakenly glorifies one half of humanity. While simultaneously lifting up women's relational skills, a theologian of the cross must also affirm the reality of trials and temptations in women's lives, acknowledging that "even the power of relationships can break."[43] Women often suffer not only the pain of broken relationships, but also the burden of responsibility for healing and mending them. Rebecca Frey's reaffirmation of female sinfulness encourages a feminist theologian of the cross to acknowledge the reality of trials, and the reality of *Anfechtung* in women's lives as we attempt to prove our own worthiness before God. But in her alternative to a Lutheran concept of sin, Hampson disagrees, suggesting that feminism can empower women to live essentially without trials. Christian feminist ethicist Sally Purvis casts doubt on this optimism regarding a secular feminist soteriology:

> One of the more frustrating aspects of being involved in feminist groups is the extent to which, for all of the revolutionary rhetoric, they mimic the very oppressive structures they seek to overcome. Commitments to cooperate degenerate into attempts to dominate, the common good is lost in cliques, horizontal violence abounds as the powerless attack one another, and the most commonly shared experience can be a sense of betrayal.[44]

Purvis's point is by no means antifeminist. In fact, this intrafeminist critique has been deepened and intensified by black feminist bell hooks, who names the ways in which privileged white women call violence "horizontal" instead of attending to the persistent vertical violence of race, class, and sexuality.[45] Another crucial component to Purvis's argument is the assertion that systems of oppression visible within the women's movement do not begin or end there. Purvis's testimony lends credence to the cross-centered affirmation that all human beings are ensnared in a complex web of sin and are continuously subjected to the temptation to replicate patterns of domination. Women are tempted to sin through the abuse of power, and they do undergo the trials of broken, wounded relationships. Locating sin and its accompanying *Anfechtung* within the female self will allow us to call women to account for their personal sin, as well as for their collusion with sinful structures external to the self. Put another way, "woman" can and does occupy the space of Luther's sinner.

Therefore, Luther's admonition against the self's preoccupation with itself need not be viewed as wholly negative or as applicable to masculine identity alone. Luther insisted that the self and its preoccupation with worldly concerns needs to die—to be crucified—in order for a new, free self to rise in its place. In contemporary theological terms, female selves need to be freed from the patriarchal expectation that they sacrifice themselves on behalf of others, or from the glory theology assumption that they are capable, in collusion with other women, of healing all broken relationships, sustaining all healthy ones, and nurturing all those who need it.

What liberation from the old self does, in Luther's terms, is create a "freedom from/freedom for" dialectic. On the one hand, the self is liberated from old patterns of behavior. The radical implication of Christian freedom, Luther proclaimed, is that if one lives a life of faith, there is "no prescription of how to act."[46] For contemporary women, this idea of freedom from scripted roles and patterns of behavior can have as radical an impact as it did during Luther's time. But the second half of the dialectic calls for a "freedom for" living for God. Luther described this as "humbly serving God by serving the neighbor." Feminists have been skeptical of this focus on humility, for it seems to advocate the very selflessness feminists decry. The concept of humility is central to a theology of the cross because it points to the power of God to transform and liberate the lives of individual Christians. Humility is not an "act" to be accomplished (as in an "act" of selflessness); rather, humility refers to a state of being in which a person no longer defines herself primarily in temporal or societal terms. A humble person allows herself to be defined only by God, who created, loves, and sustains her. Indeed, Luther's rediscovery of this radical edge to the gospel's message of freedom can have salience for women today.

Structural Sin, Suffering, and the Sinned Against

But a deeper issue still lurks within these critiques of Luther's concept of sin. Feminist theologians lift up not merely a generic notion of "woman," but also a notion of woman as one whose life has been shattered by experiences of abuse and oppression. How does the theologian's task change if her lens is refocused not on the perspective of the "sinner," but on the lived reality of those who are gravely sinned against? From the vantage point of the shattered self, Serene Jones evaluates Luther's story of justification, noting that the first scene in the drama—and indeed in Luther's theology of the cross—depicts God's wrath fully undoing (crucifying) the subject. This drama begins with a harsh movement against "the pretensions and self-definition and pride," which results in the "fragmentation" of the arrogant self. In assessing this drama through a feminist lens, Jones asks, "What happens to the woman who enters this tale having spent her life not in the space of narcissistic self-definition but in the space of fragmentation and dissolution?"[47] She suggests that one of two possibilities occurs. In the first scenario, Luther's narrative falls on deaf ears; the story is so foreign that the woman cannot see herself present in it or identify with its masculine patterns. In the second, more pernicious course of events, this woman adopts the narrative as her own story, taking upon herself "a script designed for the prideful sinner." She then will likely "recapitulate the dynamics of her oppression and self-loss."[48] If she adopts the misdiagnosis of her condition, we are back to feminist concerns over the misappropriation of the cure.

In Luther's cross-centered vision, "being a Christian is to have to suffer." Luther also leveled attacks on the structures and institutions of medieval Christendom, which he claimed caused undue suffering on the part of Christians who filled the pews. While feminists find affinity with Luther's critiques of ecclesial structures, his support of unjust societal structures deepens the rift. Indeed, Luther spoke about the relative unimportance of existing injustices embedded within the temporal realm. He called the injustices "God's punishment," insignificant because they affect only the body, leaving the soul untouched. During the 1525 uprising in which peasants, using a version of Luther's vision of Christian freedom, demanded temporal justice, Luther berated them, telling them to "suffer one hundred deaths" before rising up against the structures that oppressed them.

This fixation on the necessity of human suffering has caused many feminists to reject traditional theological speech about suffering. Rebecca Parker and Joanne Carlson Brown, in their now-famous essay on the abusive nature of Christian theology, call for a rejection of all positive views of suffering within Christian speech and practice.[49] Parker continues this theme when she writes of the image of the good Christian woman communicated to her through her own upbringing:

"She lives for the other, unselfishly. Her own needs and wants are irrelevant to love. She bears pain silently."[50] Can Luther's drama of being brought low by the cross stretch to fit a conception of sin as harm done by others?[51]

To respond, a theologian of the cross must distinguish among different kinds of suffering. Does a cross-centered approach prescribe suffering to Christians? Recall Luther's concern with *description* rather than *prescription* of the situation in which humans find themselves. At the heart of Luther's cross-centered vision was the rejection of the way in which "bearing the cross," as prescribed by medieval Christendom, had lost its rootedness in biblical narrative. Suffering under one's own cross should never become a human invention, a technique, or a work. Christians are not called to sacrifice and suffer in order to be made worthy before God. This is the religious vision Luther experienced and denounced as virtually unbearable; it is precisely the vision he came to reject through his theology of the cross.

In his recent book on Luther, Gerhard Forde claims that what theologians say about suffering is often faulty speech by theologians of glory. That Parker and Brown say that suffering is never redemptive is surely shortsighted, Forde argues, because living, loving, caring, being concerned with others will inevitably entail suffering.[52] Luther speaks primarily of the spiritual suffering we experience in light of God's work "against the presumption of our work." We want to heal ourselves, work out our own salvation. But Luther's talk of suffering echoes the Psalmist's lament of bottoming out, and acknowledges our inability to heal or save ourselves.

But the nature of suffering is not so easily resolved. While Luther talks of the spiritual, existential suffering that ultimately justifies and offers new life to sinners, does a cross theology offer adequate resources to resist those structures and perpetrators of violence that inflict unbearable pain on their victims? In her horrifying account of being repeatedly raped by her neighbor as a young girl, Parker states, "What my community could not name it could not see. And what the community could not see, I could not integrate. My religious community, most of all, could not see violence against children because it could not name clearly the violence that happened to Jesus."[53] The sickening experience of violence

and the decades spent suffering from its effects have led Parker and others to reject theological attempts to give meaning to Christ's anguish and
suffering on the cross. Does this mean that a theology of the cross and
its subsequent endorsement of certain suffering is only for those who
have escaped the clutches of such traumatic events?

A Way Forward

Sometimes I think this is what it does mean. If one were to search
Forde's recent investigation of Luther's theology of the cross, one
might answer the question with a resounding "Yes!" Forde cannot
restrain his callous reaction to contemporary theological attention paid
to "victims" over "sinners." Through a rereading of Luther's theology
of the cross, Forde directs theologians back to the "sinners."[54] But must
this be an either/or proposition? Is there a cross-centered vision that
refuses to ignore one's experiences of victimization while simultaneously holding on to one's status as sinner? Privilege and oppression
often go hand in hand. The oppressed are not exempt from responsibility for the perpetration of other forms of oppression; even victims
may participate wittingly or unwittingly in the oppression of others.[55]
Are there resources within Luther's vision that could help us move
beyond the either/or and embrace a dialectical vision that accounts for
both understandings?

I suggest that Luther's dialectical approach to human existence and
God's alien and proper work allows for a deeper accounting of sin as
harm done to others. We look to Luther's dialectical approach to Scripture as law and gospel, which he first articulated as "letter and spirit."
Gerhard Ebeling suggests that Luther realized early on that

> understanding scripture is not something that can be preserved and
> passed on. As existential life continues, so the understanding of scrip-
> ture is a continuous task which can never be brought to a conclusion.
> For there is constant threat that an understanding once achieved will
> cease to be spirit, and return to being the mere letter, unless it is con-
> stantly attained anew and made one's own.[56]

Faced with the shattered woman, then, a theologian of the cross might preach a word of comfort regarding God's presence rather than condemning her to crucifixion by the law. In Luther's biblical exegesis, for example, he is concerned about the healing of the sinned against. He affirms that God knows the victims, rages with anger over injustices committed against the innocent, and that God is the one who comforts the wounded, the shattered, as a mother comforts her child.

These aspects of Luther's thought coincide with Serene Jones's vision of retaining Luther's justification drama without having it further damn the crucified woman. Jones suggests that a person reeling from the effects of sin done against her should enter the drama in a different scene, namely, in the one in which she becomes a new creation. Jones argues that "this inversion does not replace or destroy the logic of justification; narrating the story of a sturdy and resilient new creation before turning to the moment of dismantling and forgiveness simply allows the most problematic aspects of justification (its first decentering moment) to be tempered."[57]

This inversion helps preserve what I find at the heart of Luther's cross theology: a clarity and conviction that can only be spoken from the resurrection side of the cross. For Luther this vision emerges alongside his intensely personal experience of being saved by the Word of God spoken through the cross of Christ. Could Luther's claim in thesis 18 of the *Heidelberg Disputation*—that one receives grace only in despair—be repositioned as the word of hope a cross theologian preaches against the despair inflicted by external oppression? We must state clearly that the condition of despair is interpreted descriptively rather than prescriptively. We must also remember that Luther's story is at once a personal and a corporate story. In reply to any exhortation that women embrace suffering as a means to God, a cross theologian must condemn those words as nothing more than glory theology. And finally we cannot forget Luther's dialectical approach to Scripture as law and gospel. In light of Luther's relationship to the biblical narrative, I propose that the first word a feminist theology of the cross will speak to the wounded, the vulnerable, the oppressed, is the spirit, the gospel, the word of hope, without losing sight that each life must also inevitably undergo the undoing by the letter, the law, of any and all attempts at self-sufficiency before God.

Interrogating the Male Savior

If feminists question the male identity of Luther's sinner, it is not surprising that they also question the meaning of Jesus's maleness. Let us now investigate the difference Jesus's maleness has made to Christian understandings of Jesus Christ as the savior of all. Several years ago I led a series of adult forums on Luther and feminist theology at a Lutheran church in New England. During one session, I asked participants to talk about how they imagine God. After several people offered images of God as a force, a feeling, and a presence, one woman, unable to contain herself any longer—and undoubtedly dubious about where a forum on feminism would lead—blurted out, "But Jesus was a man, and you can't do anything about that." For this woman, God's identity is portrayed decisively by *his* male embodiment in the person of Jesus.

How important is Jesus's maleness? Daphne Hampson meditates on both the great variety and the stunning similarities of depictions of Jesus as the Christ throughout Christian history:

> [The text,] *On Friday Noon*, shows illustrations of Christ crucified, drawn from all cultures and times of history. The variety is fascinating. There are yellow Christs and brown Christs, Christs who are serene and Christs in agony, Christs who are stylized and Christ in the image of the people who depicted him. But one thing these pictures—which reflect a spectrum of human art and imagination—have in common: they are all images of a man. . . . However Christ is understood, as people take him up into their culture, or make of him what they will, they know him to be male. A woman is the "opposite" to Christ in a way in which someone of another race is not.[58]

Hampson's story, coupled with my own, draws attention to the significance of Jesus's maleness to the Christian imagination. But is not a central affirmation of traditional Christology that Jesus is fully God and fully "man," that his humanity rather than his maleness is what really counts? Does Jesus's maleness ultimately carry with it a theological or, even more importantly, a soteriological meaning?

Digging deeply into the biblical/historical tradition, feminist theologians have uncovered damaging implications for women of the male savior who stands at the center of the tradition: first, with respect to what Jesus's maleness says about God, and second, with respect to what Jesus's maleness says about male (and, subsequently, female) roles in church and society. The fundamental points of agreement for Christians at the Chalcedonian Council of the fifth century was that Jesus Christ is fully human and fully divine, with no mixing, no confusion of the two natures. What feminist theologians demonstrate, however, is that there has been considerable "leakage of Jesus' human maleness into the divine nature, so that maleness appears to be the *essence* of the God made known in Jesus Christ."[59] The historical particularity of God made flesh—God as man—is the primary tangible, visible image of who God was, and is, among us. In essence, "You can't do anything about that." Jesus is male; therefore, the argument goes, God is also male, or at the very least honors maleness.

If God and maleness are somehow intrinsically related, this belief carries with it drastic implications for the roles and positions of men and women. To cite just one example, the Catholic church continues to make Jesus's maleness the centerpiece of its defense against the ordination of women. Simply put, men "naturally resemble" Christ and therefore are the only proper representation of the high priest, Jesus Christ. If the role of Christ "were not taken by a man . . . it would be difficult to see in the minister the image of Christ. For Christ himself was and remains a man."[60] Elizabeth Johnson contends that this particular argument—that only men bear the *imago Christi*, the image of Christ—is based on a dualistic anthropology that places women and men in opposition.[61] In other words, women's "natural" embodied dissimilarity to Christ effectively shuts them off from God. The only way to God, then, is through a man. The central Christian affirmation that human beings are created *imago Dei*, in the image of God, is rendered only a half-truth. We begin to see how Mary Daly arrives at her claim that "If God is male then the male is God." Such a perspective undergirds the entire patriarchal church hierarchy, and it also undermines women's salvation. For what place do women occupy within a Christian vision if their way to eternal life with God is through a male savior? Such linkage and leakage between the identity of

God and the maleness of Jesus is what has pushed some feminists to reject Christianity. Hampson explains: "Once I grasped the centrality of [the male, christic] symbolism to the religion and grasped its effects, it was time for me to leave."[62]

But what about those feminists who continue to claim Christianity? Let us briefly examine three ways in which reformist feminists have reframed the person of Jesus and his relationship to the cross to counteract the theological and soteriological meaning of Jesus's maleness. First, some feminists have reenvisioned Jesus by turning away from the cross and toward the specifics of Jesus's living. Rather than lingering at the foot of the cross, Delores Williams and Rita Nakashima Brock direct their gaze toward Jesus's life,[63] on the part of the story "in between 'born of the Virgin Mary' and 'suffered under Pontius Pilate.'"[64] This approach challenges traditional notions of salvation, arguing that Jesus conquered sin in *life*, "during his relentless opposition to oppressive systems of his day rather than through any self-sacrificial experience on the cross."[65] Brock also promotes the primacy of the life of Jesus, pointing to the "erotic power" that Jesus and those who surrounded him possessed, the power that will bring about the healing of personal and communal relationships. Williams and Brock represent a trend in feminist Christology that values Jesus's life over his death. What is most important in the biblical narrative is not God's relationship to a male savior dying on a cross, but rather God's relationship to the life-transforming, human activities of Jesus.

Second, feminist theologians have revisited the assumptions that undergird traditional androcentric Christology. Elizabeth Johnson replaces the dualistic anthroplogy with what she calls a multipolar one. In other words, Jesus's maleness was but one characteristic (along with his age or his carpentry skills, for example) that made him human. A multipolar anthropology pushes Christology away from using sexuality in an ideologically distorted manner, the way Johnson suggests much of the tradition has done. In one sense, Johnson takes this multipolar understanding of Jesus in a direction similar to that of Brock and Williams; she rereads Jesus's life and actions through this new lens. Her rereading allows her to say that "a certain appropriateness accrues to the historical fact that he was a male human being."[66] If Jesus had been female, "she would most certainly have been greeted with a colossal shrug. Is this not what women are supposed to do by nature?"[67] This approach depends upon a feminist hermeneutics that demonstrates the ways in which Jesus spent his life defying the patriarchal, oppressive dominance of Greco-Roman culture. Instead of capitalizing on his maleness in a patriarchal culture, Jesus practiced a compassionate love.

Compared to the approach that stresses Jesus's actions in life, this second approach is situated much closer to the cross. Under Johnson's interpretation of Jesus, his presence on the cross represents a challenge to the "rightness of male dominating rule." This feminist reading does not attempt to back away from any theological meaning in the cross. Instead, it seems to imply that God's choice to become male was an intentional yet subversive one. Enfleshed as male, God could most effectively upset and challenge the "natural" sources of patriarchy. What the male Jesus did on the cross as well as in life is theologically meaningful in a subversive, unsettling way.

Third, feminists have made an imagistic move from Christ to *Christa*. In the 1970s revolutionary feminist Carol Christ identified women's need to see themselves *obviously* represented in the divine; her seminal piece was titled "Why Women Need the Goddess."[68] One reformist feminist response to this need has come in the form of a Christa, a female image of Christ. This name was introduced to Christian communities by Edwina Sandys through her sculpture of a female crucifix at the Cathedral of St. John the Divine in New York City. This image was designed to disrupt—even shatter—the centrality of Jesus's maleness through its visual challenge to the claim that maleness and "Godness" are intrinsically related.

Those who want to argue that the maleness of Jesus bears little theological significance need only become acquainted with the uproar and revulsion caused by Sandys's sculpture. In Toronto, another sculpture, *Crucified Woman,* by Almuth Lutenhaus-Lackey, elicited similar reactions, many of which have been recorded by Doris Jean Dyke, who listened to voices of women reacting to it.[69]

The sculpture startled and disturbed many who encountered it, prompting one woman to suggest that "a crucified woman is mocking the very basis of Christian religion."[70] This sentiment, echoed by viewers of Sandys's work, points back to the implicit theological centrality of Jesus's maleness. Again we hear the protest: *You can't do anything about that.* "You" definitely cannot portray "him" as a "her"! And again, this is precisely why revolutionary feminists call themselves "post-Christian." Christianity, they argue, is at heart—and most decidedly on the cross—a patriarchal religion; the only way to escape its damaging effects is to leave the religion and its endemic sexism behind.

But this reaction to the Christa was merely one among many. Rather than representing a mockery of Christian belief, the female imagery opened up for other women new avenues for experiencing the cross and its meaning:

> The usual image of a man hung on a tree really imprisoned me to the idea of a male God. The image of a woman liberates me into the idea that being a woman allows me to identify with God's act. Beautiful, powerful, a challenge to take up the cross and not be a passive bystander.[71]

The biblical affirmation that all human beings are created in the image of God comes through to this woman in a way that the symbolically heavy image of the male Jesus hanging on the cross had prohibited. Another woman said, "It's really something to see one's own kind up there, and to know, so specifically, that Jesus Christ died and rose and lives for me, a woman, a sinner, and somehow, once again, a believer, rededicated to Christ."[72] For this woman, the sculpture offered a fresh vision of God becoming flesh, suffering and dying on the cross. For yet another woman, the image bridged the gap between the historical Jesus on the cross and the very real lives of women today. "[The sculpture] says something radical, something incarnational. Christ's suffering on the cross orients us to consider women's suffering now."[73]

While this image may reorient some to consider the ongoing crucifixions of women today, others worry that it raises more problems than it solves. One woman reacted to Lutenhaus-Lackey's sculpture this way: "She offers no words of forgiveness, no hope of reconciliation. There's no prophetic love in what she says to me, no words of gospel."[74] Others suggest that a crucified woman is problematic in a culture that glamorizes and eroticizes violence against women.[75] Returning again to the status and meaning of suffering, we hear the caution voiced over the contested image of a suffering woman.

Listening to the range of reactions confirms that the significance of the Christa image is much more than visual; this feminist imagining of the crucified Christ can lay bare in visual ways the emotional and spiritual effects of Jesus's maleness on particular persons, especially women. These testimonies from women also attest to the possibilities for the Christa image to expand women's emotional and spiritual connections to the passion narrative itself.

Now it is time to turn to Luther, asking, What role did the maleness of the savior play in his theology of the cross?

Feminists and Luther in Dialogue

I begin by reaffirming the obvious, that Luther was a product of sixteenth-century Europe, where commonly held convictions included an almost unquestioned belief in the God-ordained superiority of men over women in both church and society. Luther's theology of the cross is much more concerned with the specific condition of persons before God than of the particularity of Jesus's narrative identity. That is not to say that the identity of Jesus Christ was irrelevant to Luther. He did pay enough attention to Jesus's particularity to write a little tract on Jesus's Jewish identity. While his motives were missionary in character, appealing to fellow Christians for better treatment of Jews so that they might convert more easily, Luther also pointed to Jesus's scandalous particularity as a Jewish man. Luther urged humility and Christian love when relating to Jews, reminding Christians that Jews are blood relatives of Christ, and that "God committed Holy Scripture to no nation but the Jews."[76] In addition, Luther addressed the question of Jesus's maleness when he stated Isaiah's report: "The virgin shall give birth to a son and not a daughter."[77] For Luther, Jesus's continuity with his Jewish heritage is expressed through his male identity.

Beyond the important acknowledgment of Jesus's identity as a Jewish male, however, Luther diverges from Catholic views on the significance of Jesus's maleness for gendered roles in the church. Rather than insisting on the "natural resemblance" of gender between the minister and Christ, Luther describes a minister embodying Christ orally rather than physically.[78] Theoretically, at least, Luther opened the door to the ordination of women. Even though he admitted that his priesthood of all believers theoretically permitted women's ordination, he insisted that a woman's weaker voice and stature make her less qualified for such a vocation. Luther's reconceptualization of embodiment in an oral rather than physical sense also serves to de-emphasize the relationship of Jesus's maleness to gender-specific roles for Christian women and men.[79]

While Luther may not be able to avoid feminist critiques about the leakage of Jesus's maleness into his images of God, the most interesting part of a conversation with Luther on this issue comes in response to specific feminist reconstructions of Jesus's identity. When feminists back away from the cross, it comes as no surprise that a theologian of the *cross* would grow a bit worried. Lutheran feminist Elizabeth Moltmann-Wendel argues against such a "decrucifixion of Jesus" for several reasons. First, backing away from the cross runs the risk of diminishing the seriousness of the violence and suffering of Jesus's death, which in turn downplays the reality of sin, suffering, and despair in human life. In other words, a feminist theology that decrucifies Jesus runs the risk of becoming a theology of glory in which themes of harmony and wholeness can blind theology to the visible and often horribly unattractive realities of life. Additionally, this one-sided emphasis on the humanity of Jesus distances or even removes the "Godness" of the Jesus Christ event. If theologians back away from the cross, it becomes difficult to give the resurrection adequate attention as well. Jesus becomes the ultimate human example of God's love and justice, thus seemingly demoting him from savior to moral exemplar. If a feminist theologian of the cross is going to keep acknowledging the depth and centrality of sin, then a savior—not just a moral example—is needed.

A theology of the cross that emerges after the rise of historical consciousness—not to mention after the rise of feminist hermeneutical reflection on the subversive elements of Jesus's words and actions—cannot faithfully neglect the insights Jesus's actions offer for a life lived under the cross today. In that light, Johnson's perspective proves useful to a feminist theologian of the cross. According to Luther, Christ did not dictate in a regimented way how Christians must act; indeed, Luther once quipped, "If we were limited to what Christ did, no one could marry."[80] Living in Christ, or having Christ "dwell in us," meant for Luther that the vocation for all Christians is to serve the neighbor. Yet Luther's reluctance to see "service to the neighbor" in terms of social transformation is no doubt related to the slim attention paid by him to the specifics of Jesus's life and actions. Luther's insistence that "Christ did not get involved in temporal affairs"[81] has been thoroughly challenged by the work of feminists and many others who have illuminated Jesus's subversion of the norms of his time.

Again, Luther saw that while Jesus embodied perfect fulfillment of Old Testament prophecy, his words and actions were subversive in the religious arena. According to Luther, Jesus instigated an "insurrection of the mouth" through his preaching, and in this way should be imitated as a model for spiritual and religious reformation. Luther also affirms in his exegesis of the *Magnificat* that Mary preaches the Word of God when she directs all Christians to exalt the lowly.[82] In a feminist theology of the cross, these gestures by Luther can be expanded upon and articulated in feminist terms: through his life and ministry, Jesus actively upset the patriarchal structures of his day.

There is yet another way in which a theology of the cross can pair up with a reenvisioned feminist Christology. Johnson notes that had Christ been female in that particular time and place, her demonstration of compassionate love and suffering on a cross would have been greeted by nothing more than a shrug. In other words, a woman suffering at the hands of others would have shocked few. Part of the power of the narrative has to do with the way in which Jesus, the man on the cross, challenged the "natural rightness of male dominating rule."[83] At the same time, we must not lose sight of the scandal of Jesus's particularity as a poor, oppressed Jew. In light of these interpretations, Luther's affirmation that God came in a form we could not have anticipated can be reconfigured within a feminist frame of meaning. Sticking to what is visible—the male Jesus in a patriarchal society—we can see God as hidden unexpectedly in what Johnson calls "the exact opposite of the patriarchal ideal of the powerful man." Luther marveled at how Christ "refused to use his rank against us, subjecting himself to all human conditions."[84]

Undoubtedly, Luther was referring to Christ's refusal to use his divine power to escape full entry into human existence. But when coupled with Johnson's approach, this notion can be expanded to include Christ refusing to use his male rank against us, and refusing to participate in the structures of violence that were used against him. The stumbling block for Christians, then, is not only the fact that God became human and died on a cross, but also that God specifically became male "to break the fetters of sexism by his absolute humility and liberty for others."[85] Jesus Christ's historical maleness is theologically important insofar as it upsets, challenges, even subverts any marriage of the gospel message to male-dominating rule. This combination of Luther's subversive approach and a feminist antipatriarchal Jesus comes back to challenge Luther's attachment to a "post-fall" natural rightness of male superiority.

For Luther, a cross-centered theology must retain not only the narrative identity of Jesus as a Jewish male, but also the existential import of the cross for each Christian who understands that "Christ died *for me.*" The event of Christ's death on the cross cannot be limited to a distant historical reality. Rather, the biblical narrative's portrait of Christ needs to become the narrative that shapes and directs human existence. As Ian Siggins points out, Luther's Christology constantly stressed the *for me* character of the cross of Christ. At the heart of Luther's "experiential *theologia crucis*" is knowing that "we must become Christ to our neighbor, as Christ did for me," and making Christ "personalized and present in our lives."[86] For Luther, a kind of existential unity occurs between Christ and the believer through the experience of faith.

A Way Forward

Combining a feminist hermeneutic with a critical eye toward lingering anti-Jewish biases, a feminist theologian of the cross must hold on to the biblical and historical Jewish male identity of Jesus. But how does a feminist theologian of the cross faithfully communicate the intimate presence of Christ in the lives of Christians—particularly shattered women—today? To answer this question, we must return to the original intent of Luther's theology of the cross. Luther intervened into the theological conversation of his time in order to shatter what he saw as the glorious, unfaithful images of God and "man" that were currently proclaimed. Our knowledge of God, Luther insisted, comes only in veiled, hidden, and profoundly unexpected ways through the lens of faith. That God became clothed in human flesh speaks of God's hidden presence in our world. This vision of God not only upsets human expectations of God, but it also alters the way theology is practiced. A theology of the cross serves as a critical, negative principle. To question and chip away at status quo theology and ecclesiology was, Luther believed, the vocation of all those who follow Christ.

We stand at a very different time and place. Yet I want to suggest that a theology of the cross can still be useful, particularly in a critical way. Despite the growing popularity and attention given to feminist concerns, the dominant theological landscape remains in many ways hostile to them. Echoing Luther, the critical function of a feminist theology of the cross is to disrupt any and all versions of a theology of glory that suppress and oppress women. Because the maleness of Jesus often leads to the theological exaltation of maleness, a feminist theologian of the cross is obliged to call sexism what it is: a distortion of God's hidden presence in human flesh.

In the spirit of Luther, I propose feminists resist idolizing Jesus's male identity by reasserting the image of the crucified woman as the *location* of Christ today. Once it serves the critical, negative function of shattering the male stranglehold, the crucified woman, in the spirit of a theology of the cross, can then open up, especially for women, new existential pathways and insights into the concrete reality of God becoming enfleshed and embodied in particular human form.

Let me be clear: I am *not* suggesting an eclipse of the narrative depiction of Jesus as the Christ. As numerous feminist theologians have shown, attending to the particularities of Jesus's words and actions offers a vision for a transformed existence, one that offers hope for those who are entangled in the very structures of evil Jesus lived and died to overcome. In addition, Luther's theology of the cross is inextricably bound to the gospel portrayals of Jesus Christ. Even though a theologian of the cross honors his or her own existential experience of the cross of Christ, that personal experience is nevertheless correlated with the concrete, particular narrative depictions of Jesus, the Jewish man, who is also God.

Luther's focus on how a Christian *experiences* Christ's real presence in his or her life led him to critique the effectiveness of scholastic theology when it came to speaking to the mother in the home or the man on the street. He was convinced that theology must be expressed in a language full of dramatic images that spoke to everyday persons. He also once implored Christians to "engrave the picture of the cross of Christ on [yourselves]." As contemporary theologians answer Jesus's question, "Who do you say that I am?" a wide array of them speak to the existential and even political import of Christ's presence today. Womanist theologians like Jacquelyn Grant are intent on making the gospel intelligible to black Americans. Grant's assertion that "Christ is Black" does not discount the biblical narrative; instead it reasserts Christ's real presence among the oppressed in our society today.[87] I am leery, however, of suggesting that a feminist theologian of the cross talk about the Jesus of history as a Jewish male and the Christ of faith as Christa, for the narrative depiction of Jesus the Christ reveals that the "Jesus" and "Christ" go together. Rather than answering "Who do you say that I am?" I suggest that the image of a crucified woman answers the question, "*Where* is Christ today?" The image can both judge oppressive theologies of glory and imaginatively suggest that women as well as men are fully in God's image, and capable of bearing the divine.

In a theology of the cross, the cross of Christ must remain a shocking stumbling block for Christians. The idolatrous character of Jesus's maleness must be shattered to help retain the shocking reality of God's unexpected presence among us. Listening to the recorded reactions to Sandys's *Christa* and Lutenhaus-Lackey's *Crucified Woman* tells us that a female crucifix can have this effect. The "occasion" of the male-centeredness of Christianity requires an imagistic shift that the crucified woman can provide.

But a feminist theologian of the cross cannot neglect the critics who worry about the possible sexist interpretations of a crucified woman. Does this image suggest healing to those whose lives reflect that image? Indeed, the images of crucified women[88] force us to ponder God's hidden presence, God's envelopment of human suffering, in new ways. The crucified woman yells a resounding "No!" in the face of maleness of God, in the face of the predictable sexist structures erected in the name of Christ. The image of a crucified woman startles us into understanding God's presence hidden *sub contrario*. But that image stands alongside the full account of the gospel narrative of Jesus's life, death, and resurrection. The promise that must be pronounced to and with the crucified woman is that the resurrection offers hope to the crucified, that suffering and abuse do not, will not, ultimately have the final word. These concerns and claims bring us to the final area of interrogation, that is, God's atoning work in Christ.

Interrogating Atonement

Interrogations of the significance of a male savior cannot be neatly separated from questions of atonement, of how humanity is reconciled and redeemed by God, and further, of how the cross of Christ relates to the hope of salvation and redemption. Joanne Carlson Brown and Rebecca Parker state the feminist critique of traditional atonement theories most bluntly: "There is no classical theory of atonement that questions the necessity of Jesus' suffering."[89] They argue that any traditional atonement theory implicitly or explicitly promotes the understanding of God as requiring that Jesus suffer an excruciating death in order to bestow forgiveness on humanity. This image of God, many feminists join Brown and Parker in arguing, binds Christianity to both patriarchy and abuse.

Contemplating this same issue further, Rita Brock unpacks the relationship of God to the crucified Christ, and accuses traditional Christologies of promoting a story of divine child abuse, where God the father abuses his beloved son:

> The father, who loves all creation, does not desire to punish us. Instead, the father allows the son to suffer the consequences of the evil created by his wayward creation. The father stands by in passive anguish as his most beloved son is killed because the father refuses to interfere, even though he has the latent power to do so. The sacrifice of the perfect son is the way to new life with god the father. The death of the child and the intervention of the father after the punishment is inflicted, through the resurrection, are celebrated as salvific.[90]

In this reading of the atoning work of the cross, God the father is seen as one who inflicts suffering and pain on his divine son for a sacrificial end.

Jesus Christ, Son of God, becomes a scapegoat for the rest of humanity. Brock insists that this all-too-common reading of the cross event is much more than uncomfortable: it is destructive. Parker sums up feminist rejections of a theology that weds the cross to salvation: "No one was saved by the execution of Jesus."[91] Feminist theologians reject an image of a bloodthirsty God and replace "him" with an image of God that functions more positively in the lives of women and men.

The above critiques show that theologians must endlessly wrestle with the issue of suffering. And feminists also share the fear of Holocaust survivor Elie Wiesel: that a religion that glorifies suffering will always find someone to suffer. Feminist christological thinkers resist glory theologies that valorize suffering, while simultaneously bearing witness to the sufferings manifest within our world. To interrogate atonement, then, we will look briefly at three feminist proposals for understandings of the cross that attempt to free God from preconstructed "malestream discourse,"[92] and embrace a vision of God who is not abusive but powerfully loving and compassionate.

First, many feminists agree with Brock's assertion that "Jesus's death was tragic, but it neither had to happen nor was it part of a divine plan for salvation."[93] This version of feminist Christology politicizes Jesus's life, depicting his death as pure political event. As one who threatened the Roman and religious power structures, Jesus understood the risk of being harmed because of it. Brock is clear: "[Jesus's] acts in the passion narrative are acts of impassioned commitment, even perhaps rage, rather than acts of self-sacrifice."[94]

How does this reenvisioned Christology alter the understanding of God? Most importantly for feminists, it wrenches God away from willing, or in any sense approving of, Jesus's death on the cross. To say Jesus's death was unnecessary is intended to remove God from any culpability in it, to deny that God redeems humanity through death and suffering. To uncover more about who God is, theologians need to turn to Jesus's life. For Brock, God is better imagined not as a person, but as the power of love, the power that energizes life. Jesus and his community of followers demonstrate, through their liberating acts of healing and exorcizing, that erotic power "compels us toward compassion, collective action, integration, self-acceptance, and self-reflective memory in our critical recollection of the past."[95] God is the power that pulses to and from the heart of life.

The second feminist proposal shares much in common with the first, but looks beyond the life through the death to the resurrection of Jesus and subsequently to the "imaginative space of the empty tomb."[96] Elizabeth Johnson and Elizabeth Schüssler Fiorenza stand together next to the empty tomb, where both of them reject any understanding of Jesus's death as a sacrifice. Johnson follows Brock and others in her straightforward emphasis on the political nature of Jesus's death. But she suggests that the meaning of Jesus's death stretches beyond politics:

> Jesus' death included all that makes death terrifying: state torture, physical anguish, brutal injustice, hatred by enemies, the mockery of their victorious voices, collapse of his life's work in ruins, betrayal of some close friends, the experience of abandonment by God, and the powerlessness in which one ceases to be heroic.[97]

Johnson and Schüssler Fiorenza both want to pay adequate attention to the brutal cross event, but both are careful not to linger too long at the foot of the cross. The cross and death, they quickly assert, do not have the final word in Christian speech and vision.

What does the rhetorical space of the empty tomb have to tell us about who God is? For Schüssler Fiorenza, the space created by the empty tomb allows space for women who have experienced dehumanization to make meaning, to think differently about God. She insists that God is the one who vindicates Christ as "the Living One," which suggests that the God of the empty tomb ultimately will vindicate the lives of exploited and oppressed women. In a more detailed look into what the cross and the resurrection tell us about God, Johnson describes the cross–resurrection dialectic of "disaster and love" as showing God's commitment to solidarity "with all those who suffer and are lost."[98] To focus on the resurrection, though, is to focus on the victory of love and on the fact that the one who was crucified "is not, in the end, abandoned." Unlike Schüssler Fiorenza, Johnson views the cross through the lens of the resurrection, reappropriating the story of the cross as "heartbreaking empowerment." She writes, "The suffering accompanying such a life as Jesus led is neither passive, useless, nor divinely ordained, but is linked to the ways of Sophia [God] forging justice and peace in an antagonistic world. As such, the cross is part of the larger mystery of pain-to-life."⁹⁹ The theological meaning of the cross is neither that God saves us through the passive suffering of Jesus, nor that God is merely "present" in concrete situations of human suffering. Rather, Johnson emphasizes that through this drama of "pain-to-life," God's last word to the victimized is not suffering, but life. God's presence in human suffering is none other than a resisting, empowering, transforming presence, struggling to bring what has been pushed to death back toward life. In light of this "pain-to-life" reality, Johnson concludes, "It is impossible, or if not impossible at least incorrect or even blasphemous, to speak about God's stance as other than a passion for human and cosmic flourishing."[100]

For a third angle, we turn to Dorothee Soelle, where the cross rather than the resurrection remains the theological focal point. In her work entitled *Suffering*, Soelle proposes that one of the reasons Christianity rightly can be accused of masochism is that suffering has been discussed from God's perspective rather than from the standpoint of the person who suffers, or the one who is sinned against. Soelle's task, then, is to approach Christology and the "who-ness" of God through the lens of human suffering: "If people are going to resist suffering and change the situation, they need a language."[101] As she searches the tradition, Soelle finds that Christians often speak of suffering in distorted dialects. On the one hand, they talk in terms of Jesus's abandonment by God, of God's muteness when confronted with the cross. On the other, contemporary Christianity as it is practiced often tries to "talk around" the reality of suffering, a move that tilts toward apathy: "To remove oneself totally from suffering would remove oneself from life."[102] How, then, should a Christian talk about Christ's suffering on the cross?

Soelle responds, "As pure history, the story of Jesus has no overarching significance."[103] What is significant is that "Jesus dies before our eyes. His death hasn't ended." Here Soelle turns to the existential importance of the cross. Because suffering continues in our world, Jesus continues to die right here in our midst, before our very eyes. What does this approach to suffering tell us about God and God's relationship to the crucified Christ? Rather than focusing on abandonment, Soelle highlights God's unity with

Jesus on the cross. "God is not an almighty spectator, not in heaven, but hanging on the cross."[104] Echoing Johnson, Soelle insists that the message of the cross is that God is with any and all who suffer. God is far from a stranger to human pain. But that is not all the Christian narrative offers a language of suffering. God moves beyond being with those who suffer, for the cross is but one part of the greater narrative of Christian love. God, present in our world and in human suffering, battles with us for life.

If this is the case, why not follow Schüssler Fiorenza to the empty tomb? Soelle remains at the cross because for her it is "above all, a symbol of reality." The cross is theologically significant not because it is a "theological invention," but because it is "the world's answer, given a thousand times over, to attempts at liberation."[105] The God of life is consistently driven to an execution by individual, communal, and institutional sin. God's relationship to the cross is theologically meaningful for Soelle insofar as it confirms God's intimate, compassionate, life-giving presence in the midst of real suffering. The cross is also a theological necessity for Christianity; if we run from the cross, Soelle warns, we can pretend to remove ourselves from the grisly realities of suffering surrounding us.

These approaches to the relationship between God and Christ and the cross attempt to stamp out any explicit or implicit theological linkages between God and the glorification of suffering. These feminists insist on calling suffering what it is: something contrary to God's will for God's people. How does Luther fare when placed in dialogue with these feminist visions of atonement?

Feminists and Luther in Dialogue

Schüssler Fiorenza notes some similarities between feminists and early Christian interpreters of the cross who "evoke a multiplicity of images and articulate diverse, even contradictory insights" on the theological meaning of the cross event.[106] Indeed, Luther also fits this description. In the face of the forceful and varied critiques leveled against traditional atonement theories, contemporary Lutheran theologians try to show that Luther's understanding of atonement differs from the traditional notions of satisfaction, *Christus Victor*, or moral influence theories.[107] Luther found these traditional theories unhelpful, and at times misleading, because they all assume that God requires something from humanity's side, such as payment, sacrifice, or a shift in consciousness. What is radical about Luther's understanding of the gospel is that Luther reverses the direction of atonement. The message of Christ on the cross is that "God comes to us." God changes our situation, because we, not God, are the ones in need of change. If a theology of the cross is going to hold to some version of Luther's understanding of the depth of human sinfulness, then humanity must be viewed as incapable of voluntarily moving toward God, unable to overcome its own limitations and secure its own salvation. The radical message of the cross for Luther, then, is what God does for us.

Because of God's initiative in coming to us in Jesus Christ, a cross-theologian's knowledge of God and God's relationship to human beings is a posteriori knowledge. Through faith we know that by Christ's suffering on the cross, God enacted "the joyous exchange." God in Christ actually became sin for us by becoming human and bearing the wrath of God. Luther's metaphor for this exchange is a marital one: "Christ is the bridegroom who takes on, then swallows, all the sins of his bride."[108] The exchange is efficacious because Christ stands in our place, due to his humanity. Yet because of his divinity, Christ's suffering and death are salvific in a way that ours could never be. Thus, for Luther, we are not to imitate Christ's suffering—but nevertheless, suffering often characterizes a life lived in light of the gospel message.

Another key a posteriori affirmation for a theologian of the cross is that Christ experienced extreme *Anfechtung* when dying on the cross. Luther's intense personal experience of *Anfechtung* drew him to biblical affirmations that Jesus understood what it meant to be Godforsaken. This piece of the story is crucial for Luther, for Jesus could not have been fully human or really "sin for us" if he could have escaped this basic human experience of the terrifying absence of God. This ties to another key affirmation: that the God of the cross is a God hidden *sub contrario*, under its opposite. For Luther, God's hidden presence in suffering existence only partially describes God's double way of operating. Luther's God is more than a suffering God. If the suffering God were all we had, then it would leave humanity without a court of appeal beyond suffering. Instead, "We have an advocate, but no judge to whom his advocacy of our cause may be addressed."[109] This is why, for Luther, atonement needs to be understood in trinitarian terms, in which the cross event concerns God as well as humanity. On the cross, God is Victim, but God is Judge as well. Michael Wallace offers a way to look at Luther's dialectical understanding of the cross event, in which God's proper work is hidden under God's strange or alien work. For Luther, God's proper work is precisely the self-giving for us. Yet traditional theories of atonement often fail to give adequate emphasis to the God "in himself whose justice stands over against our suffering, who hears our cry and will vindicate our cause."[110] Luther poignantly described in his Genesis lectures how God hears the cries of those who suffer unjustly. The blood that is shed by the innocent, Luther proclaimed, "does not keep silent. . . . We must not assume," he continued, "that God is disregarding our blood. We must not assume that God has no regard for our afflictions. . . . But it is surely that God is most profoundly outraged by [the sins of the perpetrators] and will never allow [them] to go unpunished."[111] Although all human beings stand as sinners before God, God as Judge witnesses each act of brutality and degradation, and condemns the sin harshly.

Have we made any progress in freeing Luther from the aforementioned feminist critiques of atonement? Part of the problem is that feminists question what Luther accepts from the biblical narrative as given: that God is revealed in the cross, and that the theologian is to use reason to illumine what faith already accepts. Luther's response to feminists cannot end there, however. We must ask whether Luther's view of God's act of self-giving on the cross amounts to divine child abuse.

In response to this undoubtedly startling accusation, Luther would reemphasize that a theologian of the cross is concerned not with speculation about God, but rather with the way things are. Luther clearly believed that when God became human and lived among us, human sinfulness (manifest in concrete ways) pushed Jesus onto the cross. God willingly stood in our place and became a curse under sin. Does that make God an abusive father? Luther explained the paradox of the incarnation this way: "The humanity [of Christ] is more closely united with God than our skin with our flesh. Thus you cannot separate the humanity and divinity."[112] Luther continued by claiming that on the cross, God does and does not die. If God actually dies, Luther would insist that it is not an act of child abuse, for God's death represents not an infliction of suffering but a taking in of suffering "into the Godhead itself." In addition, Luther himself knew that a parent's worst experience is to witness the death of a beloved child. After the death of his daughters, Luther was pulled through his own excruciating grief by the belief that comes from understanding the cross in terms of the resurrection: that "God loves life more than death."[113]

If confronted with feminist reenvisionings of atonement, Luther likely would ask, "What happened to God's wrath?" For Luther, if there is no wrath of God, there is no cause for joy in the passion's movement from cross to resurrection. A God without wrath is incapable of serving as judge, which in turn makes God unable to condemn the acts and the institutions that dehumanize women and others. Johnson acknowledges that a "traditional stress on anger within a patriarchal framework" often obscures the message of divine mercy. "But in a feminist framework," Johnson insists, "the wrath of God [is something] we can ill afford to lose. . . . Divine wrath discloses God's outrage at the harm done to those she loves."[114]

For Luther, understanding the meaning of the cross is more like looking in a mirror than it is an intellectual assent to this or that theory. Luther claimed that "Christ mirrors our sin, demonstrating what should have happened to us." Because Christ actually became sin for us, Luther asserts, we are freed from having to do the same. By stressing the uniqueness of Christ's suffering, Luther was delivering the death knell to medieval religious prescriptions to suffer in order to become worthy in God's sight. What does this mean concretely? Recall Luther's invocation of the biblical story of the woman caught in adultery. Luther focused on Jesus's reaction, noting that he did not demand suffering, payment, or sacrifice. Rather, Jesus tells her, "Go and sin no more." Luther described this pronouncement of Jesus as "laying on her the cross." To live faithfully under the reality of the cross is to live as one who has been justified by God and opened to the brokenness and needs of the world in which one lives.

We cannot forget that feminist theologians are concerned not just with theological language itself, but also with the "effective history" of the images and symbols contained in the discourse. Feminists test Luther not only on his theological claims, but also on how his theology functions in concrete situations. While Luther's pastoral, devotional orientation succeeded in offering words of comfort to those whose existence was marked by unjust sufferings, we cannot overlook his brutish approaches to the peasants and the Jews, often taken in the name of Christ. The feminist theological sensibility that keeps the suffering ones visible will help us avoid following Luther down those destructive paths.

A Way Forward

A feminist theologian of the cross cannot deny the reality of violence present within the passion drama of Christ's brutal death and resurrection. Nevertheless, a theologian of the *cross* cannot back away from speaking about the relationship of the cross and the resurrection to an understanding of atonement. However, for a feminist theologian of the cross who is committed to naming the violence toward women—violence that has been justified through appeal to traditional atonement images—a shift in describing the atoning work of Christ becomes necessary. Specifically, I propose a reenvisioning of Luther's understanding of atonement as a "joyous exchange" and its accompanying metaphor of the bridegroom and bride, and I do this for several reasons.

First, a feminist theologian of the cross is committed to calling a thing what it is. Therefore, attention must be given to the original purpose of the cross in ancient Roman society: as an instrument of torture and execution of criminals. To speak in terms of a "joyous exchange" takes a feminist cross-centered understanding of atonement too far afield from the particularities of Jesus's life and death. That Jesus was sentenced to death because of his threat to the political and religious institutions of his day is obscured by characterizing it as a "joyous exchange." A feminist theologian of the cross must employ an image that better captures the horror of the historical reality of Christ's crucifixion.

Second, to refer to the suffering and death of God incarnate for our sake as "joyous" lends credence to the claim that a theology of the cross does grant intrinsic value to suffering. To combine the concept of "joy" with images of beatings, whippings, and agonizing death softens the shocking quality of the cross: a quality that must be preserved. A feminist theologian of the cross does not want to distance herself from the reality of suffering, but she does want to take to heart feminist critiques that a cross-centered approach is in danger of reveling in or glorifying suffering. Shifting away from "joyous" retains a better sense of the costly nature of God's enduring the cross.

Third, the primary metaphor used by Luther to illustrate the "joyous exchange" is the image of Christ as a bridegroom who marries a "poor wicked harlot" and takes on all her grievous sins, thus saving her from rightful damnation. Arguably the power of this biblical image comes from the husband's gift: freely taking on all the sins of his wife, thereby endowing her with eternal righteousness. In our contemporary setting, however, much of the power of this metaphor is muted or lost altogether for women and men who cannot move past its obvious sexism. The model of Christ rescuing humanity in the form of an evil woman is an unhelpful image for a cross-centered theology with a feminist sensibility.

Rather than a joyous exchange between Christ and the wicked harlot, I propose a metaphor that better matches the sensibility of a feminist theologian of the cross. It is the model of friendship: God's atoning work for us on the cross is done through Jesus's befriending humanity. Drawing on Luther's most beloved gospel narrative of John, we hear Jesus tell his disciples that "No one has greater love than this, than to lay down one's life for one's friends" (15:13). This model is suggested in the spirit of Luther's use of various images—from the devil capturing the bait to the bridegroom taking on the sins of his bride—to convey the meaning of the cross. Luther's theology of the cross was constantly applied and adapted to various occasions, and this occasion for a feminist theology of the cross calls out for an image that will better "express certain aspects of the God-world relationship in our time."[115] Luther likely utilized the metaphor of marriage for the self-giving love that ideally exists between spouses. In John, the image of friendship explains the meaning of Jesus's life and, specifically, his death on the cross. The image of Jesus laying down his life for his friends highlights the "gift character" that is crucial to Luther's understanding of what God did on the cross. Sallie McFague points out that friendship implies a certain freedom; it is less laden with a sense of duty than marriage is (as traditionally understood).[116] Friends freely choose to be in relation to one another. Is that not an appropriate image of Jesus's willingness to give of himself? Jesus was not paying a debt to God. Jesus the Friend acted freely, giving his very life on behalf of his friends. In a related vein, Forde argues that the "for us" notion, which was so important to Luther,

> should be interpreted more on a sense of "on our behalf," "for our own good," or "for our benefit," rather than "instead of us" . . . [which is] oriented solely toward the past. But Jesus' work "for us" in the New Testament is oriented also toward the future. He died not only to repair past damage but to open a new future "for us."[117]

This image of Jesus as intimate friend of his disciples helps link his suffering and atonement to the biblical story of Jesus's life and actions. The Matthean narrative reports that Jesus's friends included "tax collectors and sinners" (11:19), suggesting that when Jesus lays down his life on behalf of his friends, he bears their sins as well. The image of friendship also points to the role that sin played in placing Jesus on the cross. Jesus's words to Judas in the Garden of Gethsemane are "Friend, do what you came for" (Matt. 26:50). Jesus's friend betrays him with a kiss. Jesus lays down his life for the friends who betray as well as those who remain faithful to him.

Returning briefly to Luther's understanding of the joyous exchange between Christ and his bride, we see that because of Christ's exchange of righteousness, "[the bride's] sin cannot now destroy her." Luther explained that the bride is now "free from all sins . . . secure against death and hell," but there is little guidance for her or for us about how we are to live in the world in response to what God has done for us. In his *Treatise on Good Works*, Luther insisted that the faith in the marriage relationship wonderfully illustrates that no guidebooks are needed in order to live faithfully. Yet Luther's critics fault him for saying too little about just what faithful living in the temporal world looks like. The story of Jesus the Friend laying down his life does not provide a guidebook, but it includes some powerful images for how we should live in light of God's work on the cross. In the Johannine narrative, we hear from Jesus that his friends are to "remain in the love of Christ," which means "loving as Christ has loved us" (cf. John 15:11-17). Here is a way of seeing God's atoning work on the cross as undeniably future-oriented. "Remaining in the love of Christ" suggests the possibility of a healing vision for those whose present reality is dominating by suffering, negation, and hate, while "loving as Christ as loved us" beckons all Christians to open themselves up to the devouring needs of others[118] and even to participate in the process of healing.

Through this exploration of the image of friendship, the "joyous exchange" metaphor becomes less and less appropriate for a feminist theology of the cross. Understanding the love that drove Jesus to lay down his life, and knowing that his instructions for life under the cross were to "Love as I have loved," Johnson's image of "heartbreaking empowerment" seems appropriate to this idea of atonement. Luther's admonition to live "in loving service to the neighbor" is deepened and nuanced through the explanation that to live as a "friend of the Friend of the world" is a heartbreaking ordeal. Jesus our friend suffers with and for us, experiencing the pain of the betrayal of friends, suffering innocently, enduring the momentary wrath and abandonment of God, again, on our behalf. And yet, in the end, Jesus the Friend is not forsaken by God, and therefore, we as friends of Jesus witness to the empowering reality of hope given us by the resurrection, a hope beyond all the pain and suffering that surround and sometimes swallow us whole.

✳   ✳   ✳   ✳   ✳

This chapter has imagined a conversation between Martin Luther and contemporary feminist theologians who share the reforming sensibilities of the theology of the cross while remaining critical of many of its other assumptions—particularly those about human sinfulness, suffering, Jesus's gendered identity, and God's atoning work on the cross. While fissures and gaps remain between these two reforming traditions, some avenues have opened for possible travel for a feminist theologian of the cross. Equipped with visions of a possible new entry point into the drama of justification, the strategic interjection of the image of a crucified woman into our meditations on the location of Christ with us today, and an atoning vision of Jesus as the betrayed friend, this theologian is poised to offer a narrative portrait of a feminist theology of the cross.

5

On Becoming a Feminist Theologian of the Cross

The dichotomy is irresolvable:
knowledge of death and hope for life both have their claws in me.
—Dorothee Soelle

ecoming a feminist theologian of the cross means learning how to live in hope. Through speech and action, we live with the hope that persists despite the presence of death and all that diminishes life. Just as for Luther's cross theology, this contemporary rendering cannot be a detached vision, a mere setting forth of more information about feminist views of the cross. Emboldened by Luther, for whom the essence of the reforming task was bound up as much with practice as it was with proclamation, this feminist theology of the cross describes not just a cross-centered vision of reality, but also a vision for what faithful living in light of the cross and resurrection of Christ looks like in our contemporary context.

Becoming a feminist theologian of the cross involves building on the power of Luther's "No!" against theologies of glory that promote easy answers, facile optimism, or a God whose presence is too quickly and too definitively identified as singularly with us and for us. As I argued in part one, Luther's rendering of cross theology carries with it the capacity to flesh out the "Yes!"—the real life of faith that follows the dying and rising with Christ and his cross. As Luther suggested, receiving the gift of faith does not change the human condition with one stroke; instead a new relationship to one's condition is created by faith.[1] Even though Luther's critique often outstripped his articulation of what justified existence looks like, the dynamic tension embedded within the faithful person's status as *simultaneously* justified and sinful stands ready for expansion by a feminist theologian of the cross. The gift of faith offers human beings the possibility of *becoming* theologians of the cross, freed up to live with—and even against—the sin that continues to pervade human lives.[2] A feminist theologian of the cross understands that the critique of any and all glory theology always contains a critique of injustices that extend beyond ecclesial walls into social structures, meaning that a political theology of the cross is a necessary and in many ways inevitable extension of the reformer's theology of the cross.

Luther set forth at Heidelberg a vision of what happens to human beings, chronically predisposed to sin, in their existential encounter with the death and resurrection of Christ. A feminist theology of the cross tells a similar story from a very different place and time. This story is about a theologian making sense of the cross's claim on her and others' existence in a way that honors the insights of both feminist and Lutheran commitments. To tell such a story, one Lutheran feminist has noted, requires "a reformulation of Lutheran categories . . . to express clearly what the gospel says to us in our particular time and place, particularly in the lives of women."[3] This is what it takes to bridge the divide. The gospel message, that which is preached through the pain-to-life drama of Jesus's life, death, and resurrection, is a message not just about suffering and death but of new life. All who witness the gospel proclamation should hear the expression of a bare hope spoken through the cross, declaring—despite mountains of evidence to the contrary—that death, suffering, pain, and destruction will not ultimately prevail.

Yet a theologian of the cross knows that the gospel cannot be proclaimed without first hearing the negative judgment of the law. For myself—a white North American Christian of great privilege, relative to others across the globe[4]—and others like me, the word of judgment breaks in to our comfortable versions of faithfulness, working against a theology that embraces gospel without attending to the role of the law. The law of judgment works to break our stubborn ignorance of complicity in structures that harm, oppress, and disempower others both near and far. The cross precedes the saving gospel message of God's resurrecting work in and through the world. A feminist theologian of the cross hangs on to this inseparability of law and gospel, of judgment and justification, in a way that preaches hope to victims, to perpetrators, to all who experience the diminishment that is part of finite existence.

The feminist theology of the cross set forth here emerges out of an embrace of Luther's dialectical understanding of law and gospel, judgment and justification, death and resurrection, suffering and hope, while simultaneously reformulating the categories in which the dialectic is presented. We begin with the Genesis narrative of Sarah and Hagar and its vivid illustration of cruciform existence, moving then to the view of victimization emerging from the crucified and risen Christ. We conclude with a vision of justified existence that turns toward hope in the vocation embodied in a theological understanding of friendship.

Describing the Human Condition

In setting forth a feminist theology of the cross, we recall Luther's propensity for living among biblical characters, especially his predecessors in a cross-centered faith, reaching all the way back to the earliest chapters of Genesis and the patriarch Abraham. Luther's theology conformed to the shape of his biblical exegesis, taking on not only a Pauline sensibility, but also an undeniably Hebraic quality in his understanding of humanity's condition and its relationship with God.[5] In particular, the life of the patriarch Abraham represented to Luther, as he did to Paul, rich soil for cultivating the issues at the heart of a theology of the cross. A feminist theologian of the cross shares Luther's interest in the Old Testament narratives, in which the lives of the faithful may be decidedly broken, even cruciform, in character. A feminist theologian of the cross accompanies Luther into that Old Testament world, attending in particular to the lives of the matriarchs, the spiritual ancestors of Jews and Christians alike. If Abraham stands as preeminent spiritual ancestor for Luther—and indeed for countless Jews, Christians, and Muslims—the richly complex narrative of Sarah and Hagar, both wives of Abraham, also inspires reflection on cruciform existence. In this story, whispers of bare hope are heard amid the unsentimental realities of disappointment, pain, suffering, and even abuse.

Hidden within the drama of the patriarch Abraham is the story of Sarah and Hagar, a tale that resists tidy, static categorization of persons as either pure oppressor or pure victim. It shows that violence toward women is not simply experienced vertically, with men as perpetrators; it travels both vertically and horizontally within women's relationships with one another and with their offspring. Women too are separated by differences such as class and ethnicity that hinder solidarity. Sarah and Hagar demonstrate the broken reality of women's relationships while also speaking of divine blessing, survival, and hope.

Through exegesis of the story of Sarah and Hagar, a feminist theologian of the cross seeks to call a thing what it is and avoid the temptation to exalt one of these women in a way that necessarily denigrates the other.[6] For Luther, the contrast was clear: Sarah is faithful and obedient to God while Hagar's disobedience reveals her lack of faith. More recently, Christian feminists and womanists have hailed Hagar as an oppressed heroine while casting Sarah in the role of privileged female who colludes with oppressive social systems.[7] A cross-centered dialectical approach follows the lead of recent Jewish feminist exegesis that holds the two in a kind of unifying tension, acknowledging the sins and blessings of each.[8] Careful attention must be paid to both characters in order to understand more fully the portrait of human existence they create, one where women's agency and victimization are woven tightly together. We turn now to Sarah and Hagar.

Sarah and Hagar: Spiritual Ancestors of a Feminist Theologian of the Cross

We are introduced to Sarah when she becomes Abraham's wife. We are told immediately of Sarah's barrenness, which exists in tension with the repeated reference in the narrative to God's promises to Abraham's descendants, who are to become a great nation. Shortly after marriage, Abraham and Sarah move from their homeland and embark on a journey toward Canaan, in response to God's promise of land to Abraham. Due to famine, however, they end up in Egypt. While attention is frequently given to the ways in which Sarah—with God on her side—lords over Abraham (which we will address presently), less attention is given to Abraham's handing over of his wife—presumably for sexual services—first to Pharaoh and later to another ruler in hopes that he will be treated well in return (cf. Gen. 12:10-20). The narrative depicts Abraham as frightened by his wife's beauty, so he offers Sarah to Pharaoh in order to gain favor with the ruler (12:11-15). But Pharaoh, upon realizing who she is, chastises Abraham for letting him take Sarah "as his wife" (12:19), and returns her to Abraham. At this point in the story, Sarah is not only a woman displaced from her homeland and without a promised child, but she is also portrayed as a kind of commodity, traded back and forth between men.

Reading on in the narrative, we hear that despite God's promises to Abraham, Sarah remains barren into old age. Just as Abraham gives Sarah over to Pharaoh for his own benefit, so Sarah eventually gives over her slave, Hagar, to Abraham so that Sarah may obtain children by her (16:2). Abraham complies, and his union with Hagar results in pregnancy. As Hagar carries Abraham's child, she "looked with contempt upon her mistress" (16:4). Why the enmity? Opinions vary; some exegetes suggest Hagar possesses a pride over her pregnancy in contrast to her mistress's barrenness,[9] while others posit that Hagar resents Sarah for forcing her into a sexual relationship with Abraham.[10] In response to this rift, Sarah demands that Abraham deal with Hagar, but Abraham refuses to get involved, telling Sarah to "do to her as you please" (16:6). Sarah then "deals with her harshly," and Hagar flees—pregnant and without resources—into the desert.

Out in the desert, an angel of the Lord visits Hagar. In her exchange with the angel, we see that in the midst of the wilderness, God hears the cries of an Egyptian slave woman. Moreover, although Sarah refers to Hagar only by her slave status, God calls Hagar by name (16:8), connoting a relationship of care between God and Hagar. Also worth noting is the parallel that exists between Hagar's naming of the well at the site of her encounter with God, and Abraham's naming of the well of Beersheva (21:31), as well as his naming of the mount after Isaac has been spared as a sacrifice (22:14).[11] Both characters are given the power to name the place where God encounters them. And while the narrative contains surprising and even shocking instances of God favoring this cast-off slave woman, there are other instances of God's strange work as well. When we move to the angel's instructions to Hagar, for instance, we hear the angel tell her to "return to [her] mistress, and submit to her" (16:10). The angel's words send danger signals to feminists suspecting a sexist agenda, and yet a feminist theologian of the cross acknowledges that given Hagar's helpless condition in the desert, her only realistic hope for survival is to return to Abraham and Sarah and the basic resources life with them offers. But before we draw conclusions regarding Hagar's fate, we hear the angel bestow on her a promise similar to the promise given Abraham (compare 16:11-12 with 17:2-6). The promise declares that Hagar's son will also produce a nation; however, this promise also begins to sound more like a curse in the strife it forecasts for this son's existence. Yet it remains significant that Hagar's slave status seems to have no bearing on her worthiness as bearer of divine promise.[12] In fact, Hagar is the only woman in the Bible to receive a promise that she, through her son, will become a great nation.[13] But within this instance of cruciform existence, the affirmation is hidden within the negation: the promise, though laced with strife, assures survival for Hagar's unborn son, and suggests that he will live in freedom.

In his commentary on Hagar's exchange with the angel, Luther was convinced that the angel's instruction was evidence of God's respect and support for domestic hierarchy and order. To be faithful meant to submit to your given status in society. A feminist theologian of the cross calls Luther's sexism what it is, along with his failure to imagine more fully the consequences of experiences of freedom on social oppression and on hope for social liberation. Throughout much of his life as a theologian of the cross, Luther's obedience to the Word of God translated into disobedient stances before ecclesial and even civil authorities when he believed their authority countered God's Word. When interpreting Hagar's disobedience, Luther viewed God's Word as undergirding the hierarchical orders of creation to which all human beings, he believed, must submit. As feminists have shown, however, wedding disobedience to sin can have damning implications for women such as Hagar who bear the psychological, spiritual, or physical marks of abuse.[14] Faithful obedience for these women too often translates into remaining within an abusive cycle. Does Hagar return to a role of obedience to Sarah? To God?

The story fails to provide clear answers to such questions. We do know that shortly after Hagar returns to Abraham and Sarah, she gives birth to a son, Ishmael. But Hagar's role as handmaiden used to produce an heir for Sarah is called into question when Sarah's plan to take this child as her own never materializes. Hagar is not separated from her child, and apparently raises him as her own son. The text is unclear as to why this is, but it suggests the beginning of a change in Hagar's status as mere slave of Sarah. It is also worth mentioning that Hagar is never cast in the role of servant within the remaining narrative; for instance, when three visitors seek out Abraham and Sarah, it is Sarah and Abraham rather than Hagar who prepare food for these visitors (18:6-8). The narrative is also silent on the dynamics of Hagar's relationship with Sarah during these early years of Ishmael's life. What we do hear about is Abraham again giving Sarah over to another ruler, Abimelech, who also deciphers Sarah's status as Abraham's wife (20:1-7). Again Abraham is chastised for his deceptive practice, and once more Sarah is returned to him. Sarah, guilty on the one hand of victimizing Hagar, is also a victim herself, offered as a sacrifice to secure protection for husband.

After Sarah's return, and some fourteen years after the birth of Ishmael, she gives birth to Isaac, the promised son. When Isaac is still young, Sarah observes interactions between her son and Ishmael that prompt her to demand again that Abraham send Hagar away, this time with her son in tow. Abraham is greatly grieved by this demand, "on account of his son" (21:11). But in a disturbing twist, God sides with Sarah, telling Abraham, "Do as she tells you" (21:12). Banished to the desert a second time, Hagar is despondent, and removes herself from her son, so as to not witness his suffering and likely death. But a second time Hagar is visited by an angel of God, who reassures her that she and her son will survive. God also provides water to them both, and they persevere, in spite of the bleak circumstances.

The narrative concludes with Hagar no longer a slave; she even takes on the unexpected and possibly problematic role of choosing a wife for her son "from the land of Egypt" (21:21), which stands in contrast to the self-choice of Isaac's sons, Jacob and Esau.[15] This concluding glimpse of Hagar adds another layer of complexity to her biblical portrait, perhaps casting her as an overprotective parent who refuses to acknowledge the adult status of her own son. Any attempt to view Hagar flatly as victim, as only acted upon, is compromised by this concluding image of her as parent. As Hagar disappears from the narrative, so too does Sarah, until we hear of Sarah's death in Genesis 23. But we know that the fates of Sarah's and Hagar's descendants intertwine, and the tables turn when the Israelites become enslaved to the Egyptians.

The story of Sarah and Hagar informs the cross-centered claim that the hidden, subversive presence of God emerges in the most unexpected of places. In a poor, pregnant handmaiden, whom Luther and countless others have chastised for her disobedience, we have a vivid image of a person deemed wretched by societal standards, met by God, and given a divine promise. In Sarah we also encounter a woman who is blessed in spite of her harsh treatment of Hagar; she is a woman who wields power over the patriarch, Abraham, despite her own experiences of being given over as a commodity to more powerful men. The biblical narrative—particularly the Old Testament of which Luther himself was so fond—depicts human lives—and here we can add, women's lives in particular—as fraught with ambiguity, with God's often hauntingly hidden presence in the midst, at times counseling submission and at others bestowing bewildering promises on those believed unworthy. And, as Luther repeatedly emphasized, this hidden presence of God inevitably leads to anxiety among those struggling toward faithful existence before God.

Just as Luther pointed to the *Anfechtung* inevitably experienced by Abraham as he marched Isaac toward his supposed death, so too does a feminist theologian of the cross contemplate the existential state of Sarah and Hagar: How must Sarah have anguished as she was confronted with decades-long barrenness that stood in opposition to the promise given Abraham? How distraught must Hagar have been in her banishment to the desert, where death seemed imminent, and then in being ordered to return to a situation fraught with danger for her? What do these conditions say about the God before whom these women stand? Where does that leave those of us who are claimed by such a story and by such a God? We are left with matriarchs who, as our spiritual ancestors, fail to present tidy paths to follow for faithful living; nevertheless, we see a God who remains strangely present to persons enmeshed in systems created by the use and misuse of human freedom. The cruciform existence of Sarah and Hagar—both victims, but neither consistently so—is lived out with and before a God who is active yet hidden, whispering hope of promise into and through the lives of these two women.

Calling Victims and Oppressors What They Are

A feminist theologian of the cross, whose vision of humanity is shaped by Old Testament narratives like those of Sarah and Hagar,[16] acknowledges human beings' chronic predisposition to sin, but also emphasizes the already existing web of morally ambiguous structures in which Sarah, Hagar, and the rest of us live, move, and become. It is in this ambiguous climate that human beings, women and men, are morally and spiritually nurtured. Even before we are conscious, we participate in relationships ripe with occasions to become both oppressor and victim.[17] North American Christians like myself perpetuate harm whenever we purchase fruit picked by migrant workers paid at substandard wages, drink coffee grown in Africa by farmers exploited by multinational corporations, or purchase clothing sewn by women in Asia not permitted breaks in their fourteen-hour workdays. To announce our perpetuation of harm through morally ambiguous systems, however, is not to deny recognition of the ways in which we ourselves actually are and can become victims. Clear instances of victimization must be named, as we did in the commentary on the Hagar and Sarah narrative. Crucifixions of particular human beings at the hands of other particular human beings still occur with frightening frequency. The world is full of perpetrators and their victims. The challenge becomes: How does a feminist theologian of the cross describe the human condition, particularly the condition of women, that accurately reflects such a reality?

A feminist theology of the cross sees the story of the cross, as Luther did, as encompassing the cruciform lives of the Old Testament characters and their promises up through Christ's life, death, and resurrection. When we turn to the gospel narrative that carries the life of Jesus Christ through the crucifixion to the resurrection, we are confronted with a distinct interpretation about the identities and the futures of victims and oppressors alike. In meeting the Jesus of the gospels, we see that throughout his life, Jesus participated in all the ambiguous structures that pervade and govern earthly existence, including societal, legal, and religious ones. Jesus lived with the very real temptations present in those systems of ambiguity (cf. Matt. 4:1-11), and, as Luther noted, Jesus endured terrifying bouts of anxiety over God's apparent absence and silence—up to and including his bloody death. But throughout the life of the one Christians claim is both divine and human, Jesus the Christ consistently refused to don the role of oppressor or to transmit diminishment in any form.[18] He also enacted God's loving reign not only through his embrace of victims of injustice but also through his multiple acts of healing of those who suffered from the travails of bodily existence: leprosy, blindness, paralysis, and even death. Living this way, a way that only affirmed and never denied his embodiment of God's loving reign on earth, allows Jesus to occupy a unique status within the ambiguous realm of human relationships. Jesus's refusal to play by the rules of oppression and diminishment threatened those who held power within these ambiguous structures. His consistent refusal to use counterviolence ultimately led him to the cross.[19]

A cross theology acknowledges the grim reality of the cross as terrifying for Jesus, for his friends and followers, and for those who continue to follow him. Even though we must not distance ourselves from it, a cross theology must also proclaim that the gospel narrative does not end in crucifixion. In his crucifixion, Jesus absorbed the deprivation, the ambiguity, the suffering of the world, but when Jesus's absorption is viewed through the lens of the resurrection, we are met with the gospel message that human beings and the structures we have built are incapable of having the last word. This is why cross theology needs the resurrection in order to be a theology of hope. And while Luther reinstated the resurrection as a necessary element of any cross theology, a feminist theologian of the cross wants the proclamation of hope to come through even more vividly than it did for Luther.[20]

But how exactly does the resurrection help us understand the meaning of the cross? In his exegesis of the encounters between Jesus's friends and followers and the risen Christ, Rowan Williams magnifies the initial strangeness of the Christ and suggests what that strangeness means for identifying victims and oppressors today. The Johannine narrative tells of Peter's encounter with the risen Christ on the beach, where neither Peter nor the others with him initially recognize Jesus. Peter comes to recognize Jesus only through conversation with him, conversation that mirrors Peter's three-time betrayal of Jesus just hours before his crucifixion (cf. John 21). Likewise, the apostle Paul, in the experience that initiates his conversion to Christ, is confronted and judged by the risen Christ on the road to Damascus. "Why do you persecute me?" Christ demands of Paul, telling him, "I am Jesus, whom you are persecuting" (Acts 9:3-9). In order to be transformed by the gift of a justifying faith, Paul must confront in the crucified Christ the followers of Christ whom he himself has persecuted. These stories of Peter and Paul illustrate what a theologian of the cross affirms: that it is only in facing up to one's predisposition to sin, and thereby to one's victimhood, that one is given the gift of faith and hope for the possibility of living a transformed existence. And if Jesus the Christ stands as the only victim who never also occupied the status of oppressor, then the strangeness of Christ the victim pronounces divine judgment on those of us who are hearers of the gospel as well. Christ becomes our victim whenever we don the role of oppressor. But viewed from the Easter side of the resurrection, the vantage point from which a cross theologian must speak, the judgment is always enacted with mercy, albeit often a harsh mercy. Good news comes through facing our sin, our complicity, our victimizing—this is the suffering of being brought low by the cross of which Luther so often spoke—while simultaneously accepting the gospel message that our participation in such sin and suffering does not have to define us; we can even work against it.

The Crucified Woman and the Risen Christ

But what does calling Christ a victim unlike any other do to the recognition of the continued crucifixions—particularly of women—today?

Feminists have criticized talk of Jesus's suffering and death as unique, arguing that it necessarily diminishes the significance and reality of the suffering of other real human beings. But does pointing to the uniqueness of Jesus's suffering necessarily denigrate the suffering of others? While a feminist theologian of the cross will distinguish between the victimization of Jesus (as one at once uniquely divine and human) and all other human suffering, I also want to do so dialectically, holding both together in a unifying tension. The rest of us, just like Hagar and Sarah, occupy both the oppressor and victim roles. This is why any theology of the cross must preach law as well as gospel. As the resurrection encounters demonstrate, gospel is proclaimed only insofar as it comes out of the judgment of the law.

But just as the biblical accounts of Christ's resurrection encounters deal in specifics, so too must a feminist theology of the cross shun abstractions that belie talk about real persons—for victims of domestic violence, sexual abuse, or environmental degradation are much more than characters within theoretical frameworks. If we talk about being confronted by the crucified Christ in the presence of the living God, we must speak about our status as shifting between victim and victimizer, and we must do this carefully. For a victimized woman to find her place within a feminist cross-centered vision, a feminist theologian of the cross must call the victimization what it is, and affirm God's presence and solidarity with her. A feminist theologian of the cross affirms the interpretation of women such as this one who was raped at a dump after dropping off trash.

> "I lay there, wondering if he would come back and kill me," she recalled. As she lay on the heap of trash, injured and bleeding and wondering whether she was about to be killed, she had a vision of Jesus as a crucified woman who said to her from the cross, "You don't have to be ashamed, I know what you are suffering."[21]

It is a necessary moment in a feminist cross-centered vision to proclaim that Christ is with this crucified woman, just as he is with any and all victims. What we know about God as embodied in the person of Jesus Christ makes it "impossible to conceive of the Christian God as ever identifying with the oppressor in any relationship of violence. God's saving presence is always to be found with the victim."[22]

As selves who grow and become within a morally ambiguous world, the moment must also come when we see in the cross of Christ not first and foremost ourselves hanging with or alongside him, but those whom we wound and hurt, consciously or unconsciously, intentionally or unintentionally, as part of our existence in a diminished world. The crucified Christ must also be the other, the stranger, *our* victim. As much as we might like it to be, the world is not split neatly into static categories of oppressor and victim. We identify the victims, but at the same time we refuse to flatten or reify a person's identity by conferring that status permanently or uncritically. Our identities, like Sarah's and Hagar's, witness to a complexity deeper than the term "victim" alone can capture. In her meditations on Christian speech, Kathleen Norris attends to this complex notion of human existence, pausing over the allergic reaction of contemporary theologies to the term "wretch." Norris wonders if we lose a critical insight into human existence if we dispose of such a word, asking, "Who never lies awake regretting the selfish, nigh-unforgivable things that he or she has done? . . . It seems to me that if you can't ever admit to being a wretch, you haven't been paying attention."[23] In other words, "good" North American Christians, in addition to being unwittingly caught in economic structures that harm those who manufacture the goods we happily consume, must also be willing to look at our participation in relationships closer to—and even *in* our—home. Cruel words, jealous actions, emotional manipulations: a cross theology also confronts the wretchedness in our personal lives, the place where we hope to do our best. A feminist theologian of the cross pays attention to the fluid status of victim/oppressor identities, understanding that while one or the other may dominate one's existence for a considerable time, it is not ultimately definitive of that particular—or any—human life.[24]

Given this reality, it is crucial for a feminist theologian of the cross to point to the gap between our status as victim/oppressor and Christ's status only as victim. If we cannot acknowledge the varying degrees of our own complicity in patterns and structures that harm others, then our theology slips into a theology of glory that makes claims about God's endorsement of some victims and not others. Luther's insistence on the uniqueness of Christ's suffering is directly bound up with his denial of any glory theology that lays claim to the value of only certain suffering. The continued crucifixion of women from AIDS, mutilation, rape, as well as the dehumanization of those in prison, convicted of harmful crimes—*all* persist in opposition to God's reign. We come to be judged by the crucified Christ who is at some point *our* victim, because he stands with any and all who are victimized. The gospel narratives reveal that when his friends meet him as the risen Christ, as the one whom they betrayed, they experience the grace that judges and condemns that old self as guilty of betrayal, while simultaneously offering the possibility of new existence.

This is the place where a feminist theologian of the cross speaks of God's alien work. We witness this strange work of God when we confess our wretchedness, without neglecting or forgetting ours or others' victimization, and when we step into the pain of confronting our victims before God. Just as Luther insisted, this experience of despair or anxiety over our brokenness and failure to live as we might—this is precisely the place where true hope can be preached. As Williams suggests, it is in this postresurrection encounter with the crucified Christ that we learn the depth of our resistance to the truth.[25] We do not want to admit our sin, to confront those whom we have harmed, to confess our need for healing, for salvation. To be confronted with the crucified Christ, or with Christ's identification with the crucified woman, strips each of us of our pure innocence. This is not to say that victims are culpable or responsible for any particular experience of violent terror. It is rather to suggest that all of us—even those who are victims—are complicit in structures that allow the tables to turn.

Before we conclude this description of cruciform existence, where we speak frankly about our dual roles of victim and victimizer, we must resist any vision of human existence that relegates us always to one of those two roles. While much suffering in the world stems from the oppressor-victim relationship, we must also attend to real threats of nature that inflict suffering on humanity. Some disasters, such as flooding and famine, can at times be traced back to human agency. Most often, however, such disasters emerge out of the combustion of natural forces. And tragic events are not limited to natural disasters, but stretch into personal tragedies, like the death of a long-awaited child, the recurrence of breast cancer, the onset of Alzheimer's disease. Where do these experiences of suffering fit? Where is God in relationship to such experiences? Luther often referred to such suffering as exemplary of God's strange work, of a God who further humbles us through such tests of faith. These experiences of *Anfechtung,* Luther believed, were inevitable within a life of faith. While a feminist theologian of the cross agrees with Luther that such suffering engenders anxiety and even terror, she also insists that the experience leads us to the doorstep of the hidden God apart from Christ, the terrifying God to and of whom we cry out in our anguish, "Why? Why? *Why?*" Why does a precious child have to die before smiling her first smile? Why more chemotherapy? Why must I endure a gradual mental slippage away from reality?

The question of whether God sends such afflictions as tests of faith leads a feminist theologian of the cross away from the terrifying hiddenness of the God of creation back to the God mysteriously revealed in the suffering, healing presence of the crucified and risen Christ. The experience of faith in the midst of such tragedies is often the experience of the kind of anguish and anxiety experienced by Sarah and Hagar, where one strains to hear even a whisper of hope spoken from the risen Christ whose continued presence reveals God's envelopment of the deep wounds of a cruciform existence.

Turning to Hope

Thus, while the oppressor-victim relationship requires careful and sustained attention, the tragedy that mysteriously emerges out of finite bodily existence points us back to the biblical narrative and the first resurrection encounter with the risen Christ. Mary Magdalene, a devoted follower of Jesus who was present at his death, his burial, and his tomb, is the first to meet him in risen form. Reeling from shock and confusion after finding the tomb empty, Mary encounters a stranger, who asks, "Woman, why are you weeping? Whom are you looking for?" (John 20:15ff.) Assuming him to be the gardener, Mary asks if he knows the whereabouts of Jesus's body. But the risen Christ addresses her again, this time calling her "Mary." Hearing her name, Mary turns around, and her recognition is immediate. Her encounter with the risen Christ speaks nothing of the betrayal of Peter of Paul: neither confession of sin by Mary nor forgiveness of sin by Jesus dominates this scene. Yet the strangeness remains. In recognizing Christ not only as the one who was crucified but also as the Christ who healed her (cf. Luke 8:2), Mary is met not with her victim, but with her hope.[26] In Mary's turning around, in her turning from the despair of Jesus's death and the absence of his body from the tomb, is "the refusal to accept that lostness is the final human truth. . . . Mary is not dead because Jesus is not dead."[27] Mary's hope, deeply wounded by the crucifixion, is resurrected in her encounter with the resurrected Christ.

For a feminist theology of the cross, Mary's encounter with the risen Christ helps shape the discussion of suffering. It demonstrates that a gap still persists, the strangeness remains; yet in Christ's calling Mary by name the encounter not only gives her back her past, it also gives her a future where it becomes possible to live differently than if crucifixion were the story's end. For Mary, becoming who God intends her to be does not involve forgetting her past—indeed, for Peter and Paul, only remembering past betrayal made forgiveness possible. Rather, the possibility of redemption comes only in embracing her humanity for what it is and living, justified and redeemed, fully within the givenness of human existence.[28] Finally, the encounter with the resurrected Christ, the one who lost his life at the hands of victimizers, also makes visible the bare hope for those who have already been given over to death. It is this encounter with the resurrection that affirms the continuation of life even when death seems much more powerful.[29]

Indeed, as told in the Bible, these encounters offer a vivid portrait of what Luther understood as the gift of faith and the freedom for living a transformed existence. For Luther, encounters with the crucified and risen Christ should be experienced daily, in the dying to the old self and the rising to the new. We need to die daily to our own self-obsessions, to the pain that threatens to overwhelm us. And we need to rise with Christ when we are given a vocation that propels us into the depths of this worldly existence. We are called, forgiven, and given a vocation. This vocation, however, "is not simply to live in a happy consciousness of having been absolved. Forgiveness is precisely the deep and abiding sense of what

relation—with God or with other human beings—can and should be."[30]
Forgiveness that comes from Christ suggests that if we are implicated in
the violence of the cross, we are also in some way responsible for it. Contained within this judgment is the hope that can rise from taking responsibility for living differently, in embracing the vision offered us in the
forgiveness and faith given through our encounter with the risen Christ.
God's justifying, saving work is not separate from God's work in and
through creation; therefore, we are freed to live a justified, hopeful existence where we are in the world.

In the concluding theses of the *Heidelberg Disputation*, Luther spoke of
how, after dying and being raised with Christ, we are freed to look to
Jesus's life as a "stimulant" for loving action in the world. Turning again to
the Johannine narrative, where we hear of Jesus laying down his life for his
friends, we see that John's narrative lingers with the image of friendship,
and contains the commands given by Jesus to his friends to "Love as I have
first loved you" (15:12). That Jesus gives this command to the gathering
of friends suggests that vocational identity is not just personal in character, but corporate as well. Remaining in the love of Christ entails doing so
with others. In fact, one can argue that these words become the identifying marks of the Christian community.[31] Let us turn to the role and
responsibility of the followers of Christ, both corporately and individually, in our vocation of loving as Christ first loved his friends.

Embodying Christ:
Friendship as Christian Vocation

Living in the space opened up by justification given through Christ's death
and resurrection means living in freedom, called to a vocation of relationship with others in the world. While the Reformation vision of vocation
has been rightly critiqued for its uncritical affirmation of work,[32] the revolution in the understanding of vocation—as a calling *into* the world
rather than out of it—cannot be overlooked. Vocation implies living fully
within the limits of this world. "Faith finds expression in works of freest
service, cheerfully and lovingly done . . . without hope of reward," Luther
wrote. Remaining in Christ's love, Luther believed, meant freedom for the

Christian, freedom from bondage to authority as well as freedom to serve all without seeking merit.

For many Christian communities today, remaining in Christ's love continues through ministries of service. On the one hand, this service orientation deserves commendation; persons of faith dedicate themselves to binding the wounds created by human disorder. At its best, such service "has been relatively free of works righteousness, guided by a theology which affirms our *freedom to serve one another* purely because of the other's needs, not because of our need for self-justification before God."[33] On the other hand, while churches and people of faith enact Christ's love by embracing such social services, these persons and church bodies often hesitate to advocate for social change or to mobilize on justice issues. Those who embrace service "do not easily battle systemic injustice, or seek political and social reordering." They are far better at ministering to casualties than combating the root causes behind those casualties.[34]

In assessing Luther's limitations with respect to social action, critics often point both to his reliance on the language of service and to his vision of existence as lived out in two kingdoms, with the importance of the temporal realm fading behind the prominence of the realm of God. Unfortunately, a cross-centered stance has at times translated into a dualistic view of church and society as opposing forces, rather than as held together in dynamic tension. A feminist theologian of the cross highlights the whole person as present in both realms and, to avoid dualisms, advocates for reform in Luther's language of vocation. While a reformation of language does not guarantee reform in faithful action, a feminist theologian of the cross follows the Johannine shift from "servant" to "friend."[35] Jesus commends to his disciples a new understanding of their relationship to him: "I no longer call you servants, but friends" (15:5). This linguistic shift in turn affects the understanding of vocation within a cross-centered vision.

A feminist theologian of the cross appreciates the subversive character of friendship as an image for vocation in our contemporary context. As Mary Hunt suggests, "Everyone has friends, but by reading contemporary theology one would never know it."[36] Why has the image of friendship been so neglected in theological reflection, especially when it figures prominently in the Johannine narrative? One possibility is that friendship is often viewed as too ordinary a relationship to bear the divine. If one wants to downplay the seriousness of a relationship, one reports, "They're just friends."[37] Despite this neglect, a feminist theology of the cross views friendship as an unexpectedly insightful image for Christian vocation. In a society that downplays relationships by labeling them "just friends," this image can express God's hidden presence in a backside manner, through mundane and ordinary relationships.

To understand the ramifications of this shift for an understanding of Christian vocation, we must examine what the Johannine narrative means by friendship as embodied by Jesus. Again, vocation understood as friendship might seem inadequate for addressing root causes or mobilizing for battles against injustice. After all, Martin Luther King insisted that black Americans did not have to *like* white Americans in order to love them, and to work with them in building a just society. And is not friendship based on "liking" one another?[38] If we look to Jesus as our friend and understand him as having died for his friends—indeed, for the world—we are confronted with a necessarily harrowing image of friendship. If we are called to love as he first loved us, then our free choice of friendship cannot, must not, be limited to like-minded folk; it must stretch to embrace those toward whom we harbor profound resentment, even contempt.

It is significant that the character of friendship offers an ability to create unlikely partnerships among people. Friendship "has the potential to link persons who are, for practical purposes, structural enemies."[39] Friendship, as embodied in the life of Jesus the Christ, presents the possibility for relationships that transcend the structural barriers of class, race, sexual orientation, age, religion, or nationality. What brings friends together, Sallie McFague observes, is not first and foremost common identities, but a common vision that spurs dialogue and action. In addition, the reciprocal character of friendship works against the temptation (common in ministries of service) to understand the benefits of serving others in a unidirectional way. Such a perspective has damaging implications for the ones "receiving" the service: they become *the poor* or *the needy* and the servant becomes the one who gives, helps someone in need. But when a feminist theologian of the cross highlights the reciprocal character of friendship, she attends to the stories of a Jesus who embraces as friends those thought to be outside his circle of friends. Christ's acts of friendship reveal a host of unlikely partnerships, and reveal "friendship [as] potentially the most inclusive of our loves, for . . . its other can be anyone."[40] To embrace the reciprocal character of friendship with someone very unlike ourselves (a true "structural enemy") might, in the end, bring us closer to Luther's radical insistence that service to the neighbor means service to the most lowly among us—regardless of our personal level of comfort with neighbors we might want to pretend we do not have. Further, the use of the term "friends" in John's gospel emphasizes the corporate character of Christian friendship, and therefore of Christian vocation. Christians are called to be with others in the body of Christ; more explicitly, Christians are called to be the church.

Interestingly, feminist theologians have recently called for the church to understand itself as a community of friends, a vision that builds on the Johannine passages informing a feminist theology of the cross. A feminist cross-centered vision of "church" builds on Luther's vision of church as radically other than the hierarchical institution of his day. To call it a "priesthood of all believers" gives church a communitarian shape, shockingly different from many church structures of the past and present.[41] In the Johannine claim that Jesus laid down his life *for his friends,* we are confronted with a view of friendship that challenges conventional understanding. Remaining in Christ's love means not only living in fellowship with all of Christ's friends, but it also means Christ's friends can never distance themselves from the cruciform reality of Christ's risen existence. What might the church look like as a community of friends within the context of a feminist cross-centered vision for human existence?

We begin with what initiates persons into the church—baptism. Here our vocation, stimulated by Christ's friendship with others, is first given to us. We are baptized into Christ's death, baptized into the story of the cross and resurrection that promises death to the power of sin, suffering, and death in our lives. Luther stressed the actuality of death in baptism, which speaks to the new relationship given us through the gift of faith. Our self-understanding comes through our identity as a child of

God, and our vocation for a forgiven existence is given through union with Christ in baptism.

The sacrament of the Lord's Supper also binds the church to the crucified and risen Christ. A tight connection exists between the sacrament and Jesus's relationship to his friends, for sharing a meal "is the oldest ritual of friendship, [and] it is also a ritual so basic to Christianity that a case could be made that it is a, if not *the*, central motif in Jesus' ministry and in the early church."[42] Jesus's friendships often included a shared meal, culminating in the last meal shared with his closest friends. The last supper before his crucifixion, however, is marked not only by friendship, but also by betrayal. The sacrament of communion recapitulates that meal, including the betrayal and the cross, but "It does so as the Easter feast."[43] A feminist theologian of the cross emphasizes along with Luther that the sacrament of communion implies more than the subjective experience of remembering. To claim Christ's real presence in the Lord's Supper points to the objective status of Christ's presence as the risen crucified victim, the one in whom hope is also embodied. The Christ encountered in the meal is the one we encounter as a stranger, as our victim, to whom we confess our sins, admit our brokenness. The hope experienced in the Last Supper comes from standing before the risen Christ as a *restored* betrayer, a beloved friend.[44] Like Mary Magdalene, we are offered back our past as a past that does not ultimately define us; instead we are defined as forgiven, as justified, and we are opened to a vocation that calls us into friendship with any and all friends of Christ.

The church as a community of friends gathers not only for the spiritual and material nourishment offered by baptism and the Lord's Supper, but also to die to old patterns of existence and rise with Christ to new life, a life organized around the forgiveness of sins.[45] This new organization of life involves being called to a vocation of friendship, not only for us as individuals but also for the church as community. God's Word, met in the risen Christ, judges the church's predisposition to deny its own vocation as the body of Christ, as a community of friends. For the church to accept its vocation of friendship demands repentance and an openness to transformed existence.

This cross-centered vision of vocation as friendship gives us a sense of what it means to live as a follower of the crucified and risen Christ in the world today. It also helps us understand a theology of the cross as political. A feminist theologian of the cross highlights the value of the two kingdoms dialectic in its ability to relocate much of what counted as spiritual into the "left hand" or earthly realm of the kingdom, and concomitantly to salvage much of everyday living from the obscurity of the church's sharp distinction between the religious and secular realms. By destabilizing the medieval assumptions about what spirituality and Christian vocation are and where they reside, Luther rendered Christ necessary not only for justification before God but also—and just as significantly—for works of love in the realm governed by law.[46] To understand vocation today in terms of friendship, then, takes us into the depths of the left hand of the kingdom, into the depths of our world.

Living Christian vocation, both individually and corporately, means bearing our own crosses. This is not an appeal to imitate Christ's suffering or death. Rather, to be the church and to remain in Christ's love for his friends is to be called to join with those who suffer, those who are broken, those who are in pain. At its best, the church is a sanctuary for all such persons. At the same time, Christian vocation calls us into friendships that challenge our identities, both within and outside church walls. Laboring to make ordination more just for our friends who are currently excluded, working for affordable housing with our friends in the community who lack adequate housing, lobbying for systemic change in laws for medication distribution for our HIV-positive friends abroad and at home, we are called to embody the friendship of Christ. Living out our vocation of harrowing friendships leads us not into reigning with Christ but into conformity to his compassionate, healing humanity as he lived on earth. Bearing the cross of friendship in this world means that suffering comes as an inevitable by-product of such redeemed existence.

✳   ✳   ✳   ✳   ✳

This feminist theology of the cross represents one attempt at crossing the divide that exists between reformers in the tradition of Martin Luther and contemporary feminist reformers. New fjrms of theological, ecclesial, and social reform can be found when contemporary theological thought—particularly in feminist form—rediscovers Luther's revolutionary choice: to turn away from theologies of glory, beholden to gods of our own construction, and to turn toward a theology of the cross and the God hidden in the crucified and risen Christ. This book is just one voice within a much larger conversation between the rich resources of the Christian tradition and the challenging, prophetic forces of feminist theological thought. Let us not pass by this occasion for reform.

Notes

LW   Martin Luther, *Luther's Works*, American ed., 55 vols. (Philadelphia: Fortress Press [vols. 31–55]; St. Louis: Concordia [vols. 1–30], 1955–86).

TT   Martin Luther, *Three Treatises*, trans. Charles M. Jacobs, A. T. W. Steinhauser, and W. A. Lambert (Philadelphia: Fortress Press, 1978.

WA   Martin Luther, *Luthers Werke: Kritische Gesamtausgabe. [Schriften.]* 65 vols. Weimar: 1883-99.

Introduction

1. See Walther von Loewenich's groundbreaking study, *Luther's Theology of the Cross* (Minneapolis: Augsburg, 1976).

2. Gerhard O. Forde, *On Being a Theologian of the Cross: Reflections on Luther's Heidelberg Disputation, 1518* (Grand Rapids, Mich.: Eerdmans, 1997).

3. See Elizabeth Johnson's discussion of how theology *functions* in *She Who Is: The Mystery of God in Feminist Theological Discourse* (New York: Crossroad, 1993), 4. Johnson argues that theological language "powerfully molds the corporate identity of the community and *directs its praxis"* (emphasis mine). I agree with Johnson and others that we should be passionately interested in how our theology is lived out; at the same time, to determine the line of connection between theology and lived reality is not an exact science. We must leave room for the ways in which theologians (like Luther, like feminists, like myself) fail in their own attempts to faithfully embody theology as it is preached and professed.

4. See Douglas John Hall's chapter "Theology of the Cross as Contextual Theology," (pages 35-53) in his most recent book *The Cross in Our Context: Jesus and the Suffering World*

162

(Minneapolis: Fortress Press, 2003). It was reading Hall's earlier works, *Hope against Hope: Toward an Indigenous Theology of the Cross* (Geneva, Switzerland: World Student Christian Federation, 1971) and *God and Human Suffering: An Exercise in the Theology of the Cross* (Minneapolis: Augsburg Publishing, 1986), that initiated my own quest for a feminist theology of the cross. While my focus on feminism is distinct from Hall's focus on the North American context, I owe a debt of gratitude to Hall for his work.

Chapter 1

1. Gerhard Ebeling, *Luther: An Introduction to His Thought,* trans. R. A. Wilson (Philadelphia: Fortress Press, 1970), 226, quoting Luther in *WA* 1:362, 18f. (1518).

2. In speaking about Luther's theology of the cross as a new vision or a new way of imagining theology, I am building upon the argument of Peter Matheson, who claims that the reformers were fired by a different way of imagining that challenged and eventually overtook the enchanted universe of medieval Catholicism. See Matheson, *The Imaginative World of the Reformation* (Minneapolis: Fortress Press, 2001).

3. *LW* 34:388.

4. Martin Brecht, *Martin Luther: His Road to Reformation, 1483–1521,* trans. James L. Schaaf (Philadelphia: Fortress Press, 1985), 77.

5. Unfortunately, *Anfechtung* lacks adequate English translation. It is commonly understood as the experience of trial or temptation within a context of gripping fear. Grace Jantzen states it well: *Anfechtung* is the "dereliction of the absence of God which for the Christian is the ultimate hell." See her article "Luther and the Mystics" in *King's Theological Review* 8:2 (autumn 1985): 49.

6. Alister McGrath, *The Intellectual Origins of the European Reformation* (Oxford: Basil Blackwell, 1987), 40.

7. Jaroslav J. Pelikan, *Luther the Expositor: Introduction to the Reformer's Exegetical Writings* (St. Louis: Concordia, 1959), 89.

8. Martin Brecht, *Martin Luther: His Road to Reformation, 1483–1521,* trans. James L. Schaaf (Philadelphia: Fortress Press, 1985), 82. Brecht explains the extent to which Luther's own experiences contribute to his theology. For Luther, *Anfechtungen* "had to do with the deepest questions of faith, with the natures of God and Christ and with man's destiny and capabilities. Thus these experiences deal directly with theology. In fact, they become one of the sources for Luther's new theology."

9. Alister McGrath makes this point in *Luther's Theology of the Cross: Martin Luther's Theological Breakthrough* (Oxford: Basil Blackwell, 1985), 51.

10. As quoted in Ebeling, *Luther,* 58.

11. Peter Matheson, *The Imaginative World of the Reformation* (Minneapolis: Fortress Press, 2001), 28.

12. Ebeling, *Luther,* 104.

13. Ibid., 165.

14. Ibid., 156.

15. *LW* 34:37.

16. Ebeling, *Luther,* 156.

17. Rowan Williams, *Christian Spirituality: A Theological History from the New Testament to Luther and St. John of the Cross* (Atlanta: John Knox, 1980), 143.

18. *LW* 25:136.

19. *LW* 34:337.

20. Gerhard O. Forde, "The Work of Christ," in *Christian Dogmatics*, ed. Carl E. Braaten and Robert W. Jensen (Philadelphia: Fortress Press, 1984), 2:50.

21. *LW* 25:45.

22. Ebeling, *Luther*, 106.

23. Ibid., 123.

24. *LW* 25:145.

25. *LW* 25:287.

26. Mary Solberg, *Compelling Knowledge: A Feminist Proposal for an Epistemology of the Cross* (New York: SUNY, 1997), 75.

27. *LW* 10:327.

28. *LW* 31:128.

29. Wilhelm Pauck, "General Introduction," in Martin Luther, *Lectures on Romans*, Library of Christian Classics 15 (Philadelphia: Westminster Press, 1961), lvii.

30. *LW* 11:237.

31. *LW* 11:230.

32. Erwin Iserloh, "Luther's Christ-Mysticism," in *Catholic Scholars Dialogue with Luther*, comp. Jared Wicks (Chicago: Loyola University Press, 1970), 58.

33. Ebeling, *Luther*, 97.

34. *LW* 11:239.

35. *Luther's Commentary on the First Twenty-two Psalms*, trans. John Nicholas Lenker (Sundbury, Pa.: Lutherans in All Lands Co., 1903), 1:289, as cited in Forde, "The Work of Christ," 3.

36. Robert Bertram, "'Faith Alone Justifies': Luther on *Iustitia Fidei*," in *Justification by Faith: Lutherans and Catholics in Dialogue*, ed. H. George Anderson, T. Austin Murphy and Joseph A. Burgess (Minnepolis: Augsburg, 1985), 7:182.

37. Bertram, "'Faith Alone Justifies,'" 182.

38. Ibid., 182.

39. *WA* 12: 414, as cited in Wilhelm Pauck, "General Introduction," xxxix.

40. *LW* 25:198.

41. Martin O. Dietrich, "Introduction to Volume 42," *LW* 42:xiii.

42. James Arne Nestigen, "Luther's Heidelberg Disputation: An Analysis of the Argument," in *All Things New: Essays in Honor of Roy A. Harrisville*, ed. Arland J. Hultgren et al., Word and World Supplement Series 1 (St. Paul: Luther Seminary, 1992), 148.

43. Williams, *Christian Spirituality*, 148.

44. Ebeling, *Luther*, 25.

45. Ibid., 95.

46. Gerhard O. Forde, *On Being a Theologian of the Cross: Reflections on Luther's Heidelberg Disputation, 1518* (Grand Rapids, Mich.: Eerdmans, 1997), xii.

47. Ibid.

48. Matheson, *The Imaginative World of the Reformation*, 42.

49. Williams, *Christian Spirituality*, 151.

50. Solberg, *Compelling Knowledge*, 82–83.

51. Forde, *On Being a Theologian of the Cross*, 19.

52. William H. Lazareth, *Christians in Society: Luther, the Bible, and Social Ethics* (Minneapolis: Fortress Press, 2001), 118.

53. Lazareth, *Christians in Society*, 118.

54. Lewis Spitz, "Luther's Importance for Anthropological Realism," in *Medieval and Renaissance Studies*, ed. John L. Lievsay, Proceedings of the Southeastern Institute of Medieval and Renaissance Studies (Durham, N.C.: Duke University Press, 1970), 147. Spitz supports the assertion that Luther's distinctions, although they may be experienced paradoxically, ultimately unite under God's governance.

55. Lazareth, *Christians in Society*, 180.

56. Forde, *On Being a Theologian of the Cross*, 32.

57. Spitz, "Luther's Importance for Anthropological Realism," 148.

58. *WA* 2:453, 2–6 (1519), as quoted in Ebeling, *Luther*, 119.

59. Michael Root, "Alister McGrath on Cross and Justification," *The Thomist* 54:4 (October 1990): 721.

60. Williams, *Christian Spirituality*, 146.

61. Luther operated with a third understanding of reason (in addition to deeming it a useful tool in temporal matters and useless in the divine realm). Once it has been slain by the cross of Christ, reason can be put to the service of faith itself. See Brian Gerrish, *Grace and Reason: A Study in the Theology of Martin Luther* (Oxford: Clarendon Press, 1962), 26ff., and Walther von Loewenich, *Martin Luther: The Man and His Work*, trans. Lawrence Denef (Minneapolis: Fortress Press, 1986), 68ff. The oppositional form of the *Disputation* prevents this third use from appearing here in accessible form.

62. Williams, *Christian Spirituality*, 146.

63. H. Jackson Forstman, "A Beggar's Faith," *Interpretation* 30,3 (1976): 270.

64. Brecht, *Martin Luther*, 226.

65. Williams, *Christian Spirituality*, 13.

66. Douglas John Hall, *The Cross in Our Context: Jesus and the Suffering World* (Minneapolis: Fortress Press, 2003), 20.

67. Brecht, *Martin Luther*, 233.

68. *LW* 11:103.

69. *LW* 11:107.

70. Forde, *On Being a Theologian of the Cross*, 78.

71. Forstman, "A Beggar's Faith," 264.

72. Ibid., 268.

73. Ian Siggins, *Martin Luther's Doctrine of Christ* (New Haven, Conn.: Yale University Press, 1970), 110.

74. Forde, "The Work of Christ," 50.

75. Forde, *On Being a Theologian of the Cross*, 77.

76. Forde, "The Work of Christ," 41.

77. Ibid., 25.

78. Gustaf Aulen, *Christus Victor: An Historical Study of the Three Main Types of the Idea of Atonement*, trans. A. G. Herbert (New York: Macmillan, 1961), 107.

79. Pelikan, "Luther the Expositor," 184.

80. Lazareth, *Christians in Society*, 45.

81. Williams, *Christian Spirituality*, 178.

Chapter 2

1. Paul Althaus, *The Theology of Martin Luther,* trans. Robert C. Schultz (Philadelphia: Fortress Press, 1966), 27.

2. Peter Matheson, *The Imaginative World of the Reformation* (Minneapolis: Fortress Press, 2001), 76.

3. Carl W. Folkemer in his editorial comments, *LW* 31:79.

4. *LW* 31:250.

5. Luther's thoughts during that journey are recorded in a Table Talk: "Now you must die, I said to myself," Table Talk no. 2668a, as quoted in Walther von Loewenich, *Martin Luther: The Man and His Work,* trans. Lawrence Denef (Minneapolis: Fortress Press, 1986), 240.

6. See Matheson's intriguing discussion of the connections made by sixteenth-century Germans of Luther the reformer to the memory of the martyred fifteenth-century reformer Jan Hus, *The Imaginative World of the Reformation,* 30.

7. Martin Brecht, *Martin Luther: His Road to Reformation, 1483–1521,* trans. James L. Schaaf (Philadelphia: Fortress Press, 1985), 349.

8. *LW* 44:21.

9. *LW* 44:60–61.

10. *LW* 44:113.

11. *LW* 44:26.

12. *LW* 44:26.

13. *LW* 44:26.

14. *LW* 44:28.

15. *LW* 44:47.

16. *LW* 44:60.

17. *LW* 44:30.

18. Rowan Williams, *Christian Spirituality: A Theological History from the New Testament to Luther and St. John of the Cross* (Atlanta: John Knox, 1980), 154.

19. Ibid., 152.

20. Matheson, *The Imaginative World of the Reformation,* 46.

21. Forde uses this terminology in *On Being a Theologian of the Cross: Reflections on Luther's Heidelberg Disputation, 1518* (Grand Rapids, Mich.: Eerdmans, 1997), x.

22. Matheson, *The Imaginative World of the Reformation,* 27. This section on the Reformation Treatises is influenced by Matheson's reading of the Treatises and his attention to the Luther's use of imagery. See Matheson, chap. 2.

23. *LW* 44:139.

24. *LW* 44:165.

25. Gerhard O. Forde, "The Work of Christ," in *Christian Dogmatics,* ed. Carl E. Braaten and Robert W. Jensen (Philadelphia: Fortress Press, 1984), 50.

26. Matheson, *The Imaginative World of the Reformation,* 22.

27. *TT,* 5.

28. *TT,* 8.

29. *LW* 44:217.

30. Matheson, *The Imaginative World of the Reformation,* 95.

31. *TT*, 13–14.
32. *TT*, 166.
33. *TT*, 124.
34. *LW* 44:134.
35. *LW* 36:135.
36. *TT*, 115.
37. *TT*, 177.
38. Matheson, *The Imaginative World of the Reformation*, 22–23.
39. *TT*, 21.
40. *TT*, 86.
41. Matheson, *The Imaginative World of the Reformation*, 25–26.
42. *TT*, 111.
43. Forde, "The Work of Christ," 50.
44. *TT*, 172–174.
45. *LW* 31:352.
46. *LW* 31:352.
47. Forde, "The Work of Christ," 52.
48. *LW* 31:357.
49. *LW* 36:33.
50. *TT*, 191.
51. *LW* 36:68.
52. *LW* 36:68.
53. *TT*, 196.
54. *LW* 36:90.
55. *TT*, 158.
56. *LW* 31:344.
57. *LW* 31:340.
58. Otto Pesch, "Free by Faith: Luther's Contribution to Theological Anthropology," in *Martin Luther and the Modern Mind: Freedom, Conscience, Toleration, Rights*, vol. 22, Toronto Studies in Theology, ed. Manfred Hoffman (Lewiston, N.Y.: Mellen, 1985), 45.
59. *LW* 31:364.
60. *LW* 31:365.
61. Williams, *Christian Spirituality*, 154.
62. *TT*, 294.
63. *LW* 31:370.
64. *LW* 31:368.
65. *LW* 32:123.
66. Von Loewenich, *Martin Luther*, 195.
67. Matheson, *The Imaginative World of the Reformation*, 123.
68. Ibid., 38.
69. Robert Fife, *The Revolt of Martin Luther* (New York: Columbia University Press, 1957), 626.
70. For a more detailed discussion of the developments that contributed to unrest in Wittenberg, see Martin Brecht, *Martin Luther: Shaping and Defining the Reformation: 1521–1532*, trans. James Schaaf (Minneapolis: Fortress Press, 1990), 30–39.

71. Von Loewenich, *Martin Luther,* 226.

72. See Heiko Oberman's fascinating chapter, "The Gospel of Social Unrest: 450 Years after the So-Called 'German Peasants' War' of 1525," in *The Dawn of the Reformation: Essays in Late Medieval and Early Reformation Thought,* ed. Heiko A. Oberman (Grand Rapids, Mich.: Eerdmans, 1992), 155-178.

73. *LW* 45:57–75.

74. Cynthia Grant Schoenberger, "Luther and the Justifiability of Resistance to Legitimate Authority," *Journal of the History of Ideas* 40, no. 1 (1979): 4.

75. Ibid.

76. Ibid., 5.

77. William H. Lazareth, *Christians in Society: Luther, the Bible, and Social Ethics* (Minneapolis: Fortress Press, 2001), 29.

78. Ibid., 15.

79. Von Loewenich, *Martin Luther,* 241.

80. Schoenberger, "Luther and the Justifiability of Resistance," 3.

81. Ibid., 6.

82. James Wood, "Two Kingdoms—In America?" *Currents in Theology and Missions* 14 (1987): 169.

83. Lazareth, *Christians in Society,* 16.

84. *LW* 45:352.

85. I want to note the significance of Luther's insistence on compulsory education for girls as well as boys. In late-medieval Europe, education of girls was not a high priority. George Lindbeck observes that this particular reform of Luther's, carried on by later Protestants, basically assured that "modern feminism became inevitable in the long run." See George Lindbeck, "Modernity and Luther's Understanding of the Freedom of the Christian," in Hoffmann, *Martin Luther and the Modern Mind,* 8.

86. Oberman, "The Gospel of Social Unrest," 156.

87. Ibid., 161.

88. *LW* 46:17–46.

89. Oberman says of Müntzer: "He serves as an excellent illustration of the apocalypticism on the edges of the 'Gospel of Social Unrest.' Except for the last stages of the uprising, he would have remained a marginal figure if he had not been singled out by Luther for attack" ("The Gospel of Social Unrest," 172). See also Abraham Friesen's remarks: "it must be denied that [Müntzer] masterminded the revolt" (*Reformation and Utopia: The Marxist Interpretation of the Reformation and Its Antecedents* [Wiesbaden: Franz Steiner Verlag, 1974], 45).

90. Matheson, *The Imaginative World of the Reformation,* 75.

91. Friesen, *Reformation and Utopia,* 59.

92. Matheson, *The Imaginative World of the Reformation,* 74–75, relying on James M. Stayer, *The German Peasants' War and Anabaptist Community of Goods* (Montreal: McGill-Queen's University Press, 1991), 43.

93. Matheson, *The Imaginative World of the Reformation,* 76.

94. *LW* 46:48.

95. *LW* 46:54.

96. *LW* 46:59.

97. *LW* 46:69.

98. Williams, *Christian Spirituality*, 151.

99. Ibid., 151.

100. Matheson, *The Imaginative World of the Reformation*, 77.

101. Oberman argues that many peasant leaders occupied a higher social and educational status than is generally suggested. Therefore, it was not a matter of the peasants hearing Luther's ideas and failing to understand the nuances. Oberman suggests that the peasants, armed with their *Twelve Articles*, behaved similarly to Luther when they claimed "higher obedience" to God rather than to feudal lords. See Oberman, "The Gospel of Social Unrest," 161–69.

102. Matheson, *The Imaginative World of the Reformation*, 85.

103. Ibid., 99.

104. Jürgen Moltmann, "Reformation and Revolution," in Hoffmann, *Martin Luther and the Modern Mind*, 186.

105. Moltmann, "Reformation and Revolution," 186.

106. For the text of *De libero arbitrio*, see *Luther and Erasmus: Free Will and Salvation*, ed. E. Gordon Rupp and Philip S. Watson Library of Christian Classics (Philadelphia: Westminster, 1978), 24.

107. *De libero arbitrio*, 13.

108. Matheson, *The Imaginative World of the Reformation*, 83.

109. Oberman, "The Gospel of Social Unrest," 164.

110. Brecht, *Martin Luther*, 213.

111. *LW* 33:74–75.

112. *LW* 33:70.

113. *LW* 33:274.

114. *LW* 33:130.

115. *LW* 33:140.

116. *LW* 33:206.

117. H. Jackson Forstman, "A Beggar's Faith," *Interpretation* 30, no. 3 (1976): 266.

118. Ibid., 270.

119. Helmut Bandt, *Luthers Lehre vom Verborgenen Gott* (Berlin: Evangelische Verlagsanstalt, 1958), 19.

120. See Brian Gerrish's valuable article "'To the Unknown God': Luther and Calvin on the Hiddenness of God," *Journal of Religion* 53 (1973): 263–93.

121. *De libero arbitrio*, 116.

122. *LW* 33:139.

123. Gerrish, "'To the Unknown God,'" 275.

124. Ibid., 274.

125. Ibid., 276.

126. *De libero arbitrio*, 201.

127. Gerrish, "'To the Unknown God,'" 291.

128. *De libero arbitrio*, 306.

129. *LW* 33:293.

130. *LW* 33:142.

131. *De libero arbitrio*, 140.

132. *LW* 33:52.

133. *De libero arbitrio,* 140.

134. Ibid., 129.

Chapter 3

1. Mark U. Edwards Jr., *Luther's Last Battles: Politics and Polemics, 1531–1546* (Ithaca, N.Y.: Cornell University Press, 1983), 5.

2. Gerhard Ebeling, *Luther: An Introduction to His Thought,* trans. R. A. Wilson (Philadelphia: Fortress Press, 1970), 227.

3. Heiko A. Oberman, "The Gospel of Social Unrest: 450 Years after the So-Called 'German Peasants' War' of 1525," in *The Dawn of the Reformation: Essays in Late Medieval and Early Reformation Thought,* ed. Heiko A. Oberman (Grand Rapids, Mich.: Eerdmans, 1992), 172.

4. See "Luther and the Protestant Reformation: From Nun to Parson's Wife," in *Women and Religion: A Feminist Sourcebook of Christian Thought,* ed. Elizabeth Clark and Herbert Richardson (New York: Harper & Row, 1977), 131–48.

5. Walter von Loewenich, *Martin Luther: The Man and His Work,* trans. Lawrence Denef (Minneapolis: Fortress Press, 1986), 285.

6. As recorded by von Loewenich, Ibid.

7. Edwards, *Luther's Last Battles,* 113.

8. Peter Matheson, *The Imaginative World of the Reformation* (Minneapolis: Fortress Press, 2001), 92.

9. Ibid., 90.

10. Ebeling, *Luther,* 200.

11. *LW* 34:77.

12. *LW* 37:56, emphasis mine.

13. *LW* 37:83.

14. Von Loewenich, *Martin Luther,* 303.

15. *LW* 37:210.

16. *LW* 37:233.

17. *LW* 37:246.

18. *LW* 37:57.

19. *LW* 37:72.

20. *LW* 37:71.

21. Oberman, "The Gospel of Social Unrest," 158.

22. Ibid., 305.

23. Ibid., 245.

24. *LW* 34:xii.

25. Martin Brecht, *Martin Luther: Shaping and Defining the Reformation: 1521–1532,* trans. James Schaaf (Minneapolis: Fortress Press, 1990), 459.

26. *LW* 47:14, 24–25, as quoted in Robert Bertram, "*Confessio:* Self-Defense Becomes Subversive," *Dialog* 26:3 (1987): 203.

27. Bertram, "*Confessio,*" 203.

28. *LW* 34:11.

29. Preserved Smith and Charles M. Jacobs, eds. and trans., *Luther's Correspondence and Other Contemporary Letters*, vol. 2 (Philadelphia: Lutheran Publication Society, 1918), 522, as quoted in preface to *LW* 34:6.

30. Bertram, "*Confessio*," 204.

31. *LW* 47:30.

32. Bertram, "*Confessio*," 205.

33. Edwards, *Luther's Last Battles*, 35.

34. *LW* 47:20.

35. *LW* 47:35.

36. *LW* 47:51.

37. Edwards, *Luther's Last Battles*, 66.

38. Martin Brecht, *Martin Luther: The Preservation of the Church: 1532–1546*, trans. James L. Schaaf (Minneapolis: Fortress Press, 1993), 136.

39. William H. Lazareth, *Christians in Society: Luther, the Bible, and Social Ethics* (Minneapolis: Fortress Press, 2001), 38.

40. James Samuel Preus, *From Shadow to Promise: Old Testament Interpretation from Augustine to Young Luther* (Cambridge, Mass.: Harvard University Press, 1969), 203.

41. *LW* 25:153.

42. *LW* 4:191.

43. Preus, *From Shadow to Promise*, 244.

44. Ibid., 263.

45. *LW* 3:228.

46. Walter von Loewenich, *Luther's Theology of the Cross* (Minneapolis: Augsburg, 1976), 92.

47. Ebeling, *Luther*, 105.

48. Paul Althaus, *The Theology of Martin Luther*, trans. Robert C. Schultz (Philadelphia: Fortress Press, 1966), 34.

49. *LW* 1:11.

50. John Dillenberger, *God Hidden and Revealed: An Interpretation of Luther's Deus Absconditus and Its Significance for Religious Thought* (Philadelphia: Muhlenberg Press, 1953), 55.

51. *LW* 2:45.

52. Dillenberger, *God Hidden and Revealed*, 59.

53. *LW* 2:143.

54. Lazareth, *Christians in Society*, 102.

55. *LW* 1:48.

56. Jaroslav J. Pelikan, *Luther the Expositor: Introduction to the Reformer's Exegetical Writings* (St. Louis: Concordia, 1959), 183.

57. *LW* 1:64–65.

58. *LW* 2:267.

59. *LW* 1:103.

60. *LW* 3:51.

61. Mary Knutson, "Toward a Contemporary Theology of the Cross," Convocation Address (5 October 1995), Luther Seminary, St. Paul, Minnesota.

62. Rowan Williams, *Christian Spirituality: A Theological History from the New Testament to Luther and St. John of the Cross* (Atlanta: John Knox, 1980), 154.

63. *LW* 4:16.

64. *LW* 4:16.

65. *LW* 4:44.

66. *LW* 2:48.

67. *LW* 1:157.

68. *LW* 3:172.

69. *LW* 2:135.

70. *LW* 3:48.

71. *LW* 3:62.

72. *LW* 3:62.

73. *LW* 4:37.

74. *LW* 4:93.

75. *LW* 4:144.

76. *LW* 4:7.

77. Von Loewenich, *Luther's Theology of the Cross,* 88.

78. *LW* 4:62.

79. *LW* 3:72, 74.

80. Matheson, *The Imaginative World of the Reformation,* 121–22.

81. *LW* 4:57.

82. *LW* 3:70.

83. *LW* 4:57.

84. *LW* 2:319.

85. *LW* 2:325.

86. *LW* 1:196.

87. *LW* 2:143.

88. *LW* 2:145.

89. See Douglas John Hall's helpful discussion of Luther's understanding of God's compassion in *The Cross in Our Context: Jesus and the Suffering World* (Minneapolis: Fortress Press, 2003), 22.

90. Von Loewenich, *Luther's Theology of the Cross,* 113.

91. *LW* 3:94, 96.

92. Edwards, *Luther's Last Battles,* 34.

93. Martin Bertram's Introduction to *On the Jews and Their Lies, LW* 47:131.

94. *LW* 3:228.

95. Bertram, Introduction, *LW* 47:134.

96. Edwards, *Luther's Last Battles,* 138.

97. *LW* 47:138–39.

98. *LW* 47:139.

99. Edwards, *Luther's Last Battles,* 3.

100. In his lectures on the Psalms, Luther describes the Jews as "dust," "dry in spirit and abased" (*LW* 10:30). Due to their status, Luther insists that the Jews "should be driven out of the church as well as the land" (*LW* 10:166).

101. See Edwards's discussion of this event, *Luther's Last Battles,* 128–33.

Chapter 4

1. For surveys of the rise of late-twentieth-century feminism, see Elizabeth A. Johnson, *She Who Is: The Mystery of God in Feminist Theological Discourse* (New York: Crossroad, 1993), chaps. 2–4, and Kathryn Greene-McCreight, *Feminist Reconstructions of Christian Doctrine: Narrative Analysis and Appraisal* (New York: Oxford University Press, 2000), chap. 2.

2. "Womanist" is a self-description for many African American women theologians and ethicists; *"mujerista"* is the term used by Latina women to describe their theological and ethical reflections. See, for instance, Emilie Townes, ed., *A Troubling in My Soul: Womanist Perspectives on Evil and Suffering* (Maryknoll, N.Y.: Orbis, 1993), and Ada María Isasi-Díaz, *En la Lucha: Elaborating a* Mujerista *Theology* (Minneapolis: Fortress Press, 2004). "Two-thirds world" is a designation given by some scholars to all that is *not* the "first world." The phrase is designed to remind us that while the "first world" may dominate economically, the "two-thirds world" dominates in geographical size and population.

3. Carol P. Christ and Judith Plaskow, eds., *Womanspirit Rising: A Feminist Reader in Religion* (San Francisco: Harper & Row, 1979), 9–11.

4. See Mary Daly's discussion of this assertion in *Beyond God the Father: Toward a Philosophy of Women's Liberation* (Boston: Beacon, 1973), 8–11.

5. Daphne Hampson, *Theology and Feminism* (Oxford: Blackwell, 1990), 54.

6. Naomi Goldenberg, a Jewish feminist, coined this term when referring to the act of reflecting on the divine in specifically female terms. For a brief history of the term, see the "thealogy" entry in the *Dictionary of Feminist Theologies,* ed. Letty M. Russell and J. Shannon Clarkson (Louisville, Ky.: Westminster John Knox, 1996), 100–116.

7. See Carol P. Christ, "Why Women Need the Goddess: Phenomenological, Psychological, and Political Reflections," in Christ and Plaskow, *Womanspirit Rising,* 273–87 (San Francisco: Harper & Row, 1979), and Nelle Morton, "The Goddess as Metaphoric Image," in *Weaving the Visions: New Patterns in Feminist Spirituality,* ed. Judith Plaskow and Carol P. Christ (San Francisco: Harper, 1989), 111–19, for instance.

8. Sallie McFague, *Metaphorical Theology: Models of God in Religious Language* (Philadelphia: Fortress Press, 1982), 146.

9. Rosemary Radford Ruether, "Christian Feminist Theology: History and Future," in *Daughters of Abraham: Feminist Thought in Judaism, Christianity, and Islam,* ed. Yvonne Yazbeck Haddad and John L. Esposito (Gainesville: University of Florida Press, 2001), 68–69.

10. Ruether, "Christian Feminist Theology," 69.

11. Elizabeth Schüssler Fiorenza, *Jesus: Miriam's Child, Sophia's Prophet: Critical Issues in Feminist Christology* (New York: Continuum), 107.

12. The 1996 gathering of "Lutheran Women in Theological Education" at the annual meeting of the American Academy of Religion was devoted to "Luther and Feminist Theology," resulting in a subsequent issue of the Lutheran journal *Currents in Theology and Mission* 24, no. 1 (February 1997) devoted entirely to the same topic. One of the contributors to that issue now has devoted an entire book to the creative, mutually enhancing pairing of Luther and feminist philosophy. See Mary M. Solberg's *Compelling Knowledge: A Feminist Proposal for an Epistemology of the Cross* (Albany: SUNY, 1997).

13. Here I borrow George Lindbeck's phrase "grammar of faith" to describe the ongoing influence of Luther's theology on those feminists who continue to stand within

the Lutheran confessional tradition. See Lindbeck, *The Nature of Doctrine: Religion and Theology in a Postliberal Age* (Philadelphia: Westminster, 1984).

14. To cite just one example from a battered woman who sought help from her clergyman: she writes, "I was encouraged to be more tolerant and understanding. Most important, I was to forgive [my husband] the beatings just as Christ had forgiven me from the cross. I did that, too." From "Letter from a Battered Wife," in *Battered Women: From a Theology of Suffering to an Ethic of Empowerment*, ed. Joy M. K. Bussert (Division for Mission in North America: Lutheran Church in America, 1986), 83.

15. Mary C. Boys, "The Cross: Should a Symbol Betrayed Be Reclaimed?" *Cross Currents: The Journal of the Association for Religious and Intellectual Life* 44, no. 1 (spring 1994): 19–20.

16. See, for example, Daphne Hampson's "Luther on the Self: A Feminist Critique" and Mary Wiesner's "Luther and Women: The Death of Two Marys," both in *Feminist Theology: A Reader* (Louisville, Ky.: Westminster John Knox, 1990), 215–25, 123–37, respectively.

17. Delores Williams prefers "demonarchy" to "patriarchy" because it emphasizes the structures that benefit white women and men while simultaneously harming women and men of color. See her illuminating article "The Color of Feminism: Or Speaking the Black Woman's Tongue," in *Feminist Theological Ethics: A Reader*, ed. Lois K. Daly (Louisville, Ky.: Westminster John Knox, 1994), 42–58.

18. Schüssler Fiorenza also dislikes the limitations of the term "patriarchy" and instead introduced the neologism "kyriarchy" into feminist theological conversation, to underscore the pyramidal shape of oppression, and to focus on those women at the bottom of a multidimensional structure of oppression. See her description in *Jesus: Miriam's Child, Sophia's Prophet*, 14.

19. A narrative theologian understands the biblical stories as creating the interpretive universe in which Christians live and act.

20. Greene-McCreight, *Feminist Reconstructions of Christian Doctrine*, chap. 2.

21. See Brian Gerrish's intriguing chapter on subjectivism in Luther's thought, "Doctor Martin Luther: Subjectivity and Doctrine in the Lutheran Reformation," in *Continuing the Reformation: Essays on Modern Religious Thought*, ed. Brian Gerrish (Chicago: University of Chicago Press, 1993), 48ff.

22. See her relentless critique of feminist theology in Katharina von Kellenbach, *Anti-Judaism in Feminist Religious Writings* (Atlanta: Scholars, 1994).

23. The position first articulated by Valerie Saiving in her article "The Human Situation: A Feminine View," *Journal of Religion* 40 (April 1960), reprinted in Christ and Plaskow, *Womanspirit Rising*, 25–42.

24. Saiving, "The Human Situation," 38.

25. Judith Plaskow, *Sex, Sin, and Grace: Women's Experience and the Theologies of Reinhold Niebuhr and Paul Tillich* (Washington, D.C.: University Press of America, 1980). On page 2, Plaskow offers a critical appraisal of Saiving's position: "Saiving's own distinctions between masculine and feminine character was not flexible enough to serve as a consistence basis for theological criticism. Although she approached her subject by asking how men and women have experienced themselves rather than whether there are innate differences between them, she tended to see differences in experience as rooted quite solidly in biology. This raised questions as to how 'underdevelopment or negation of the self,'

being inherent, can at the same time be considered sinful and why and how theology should seek to discourage what is inherent in female character." This is precisely why Plaskow adopts a social-constructivist approach to sin.

26. Ibid.

27. Ibid., 168.

28. Ibid., 154.

29. Ibid., 87.

30. Ibid., 170, 172.

31. Hampson, "Luther on the Self," 219.

32. Ibid., 222.

33. Daphne Hampson, "Reinhold Niebuhr on Sin: A Critique," in *Reinhold Niebuhr and the Issues of Our Time*, ed. Richard Harries (London: Mowbray, 1986), 51.

34. Hampson, "Luther on the Self," 215.

35. Serene Jones, *Feminist Theory and Christian Theology: Cartographies of Grace* (Minneapolis: Fortress Press, 2000), 61.

36. Ibid.

37. Rebecca Frey, "Why Women Want the Goddess: Experiential and Confessional Reflections," *Lutheran Forum* 25, no. 3 (August 1991): 20.

38. This assertion may imply a return to biologically based notions of sin. I am not advocating for the affirmation of biologically based essentialism, however. Rather I am suggesting that sinfulness inheres in and is shared by human beings.

39. Otto Pesch, "Free by Faith: Luther's Contribution to Theological Anthropology," in *Martin Luther and the Modern Mind: Freedom, Conscience, Toleration, Rights*, vol. 22, Toronto Studies in Theology, ed. Manfred Hoffman (Lewiston, N.Y.: Mellen, 1985), 38.

40. Eric Gritsch, "Convergence and Conflict in Feminist and Lutheran Theologies," *Dialog* 24, no. 1 (winter 1985): 13.

41. See Jean Bethke Elshtain's fascinating discussion of women and men in the private and public spheres in *Public Man, Private Woman: Women in Social and Political Thought* (Princeton, N.J.: Princeton University Press, 1981).

42. See Mary Hunt's illuminating presentation of the power of women's friendships in *Fierce Tenderness: A Feminist Theology of Friendship* (New York: Crossroad, 1991).

43. Elizabeth Moltmann-Wendel, "A Feminist Theology of the Cross," in *God: His and Hers*, Elizabeth Moltmann-Wendel and Jürgen Moltmann (New York: Corssroad, 1991), 85.

44. Sally B. Purivs, *The Power of the Cross: Foundations for a Christian Feminist Ethic of Community* (Nashville, Tenn.: Abingdon, 1993), 16.

45. See bell hooks's description of her experiences with white feminists in *Feminist Theory from Margin to Center* (Boston: South End Press, 1984).

46. *LW* 44:27.

47. Jones, *Feminist Theory and Christian Theology*, 62.

48. Ibid., 63.

49. Joanne Carlson Brown and Rebecca Parker, "For God So Loved the World?" in *Christianity, Patriarchy, and Abuse: A Feminist Critique*, ed. Joanne Carlson Brown and Carole R. Bohn (Cleveland, Ohio: Pilgrim, 1989), 27.

50. Rita Nakashima Brock and Rebecca Parker, "Away from the Fire: Rebecca's

Story," in *Proverbs of Ashes: Violence, Redemptive Suffering, and the Search for What Saves Us* (Boston: Beacon, 2001), 192.

51. Marie Fortune, "The Conundrum of Sin, Sex, Violence, and Theodicy," in *The Other Side of Sin: Woundedness from the Perspective of the Sinned-Against*, ed. Andrew Sung Park and Susan L. Nelson (Albany: SUNY, 2001), 132.

52. Gerhard O. Forde, *On Being a Theologian of the Cross: Reflections on Luther's Heidelberg Disputation, 1518* (Grand Rapids, Mich.: Eerdmans, 1997), 86.

53. Parker, "The Unblessed Child: Rebecca's Story," in Brock and Parker, *Away from the Fire*, 199.

54. Forde, preface to *On Being a Theologian of the Cross.*

55. Von Kellenbach, *Anti-Judaism in Feminist Religious Writings*, 18.

56. Gerhard Ebeling, *Luther: An Introduction to His Thought*, trans. R. A. Wilson (Philadelphia: Fortress Press, 1970), 99.

57. Jones, *Feminist Theory and Christian Theology*, 63.

58. Hampson, *Theology and Feminism*, 77, referring to Hans Ruedi Weber's *On a Friday Noon* (London: SPCK, 1979).

59. Johnson, *She Who Is*, 152, emphasis mine.

60. From the *Vatican Declaration on the Question of the Admission of Women to the Ministerial Priesthood* (1976), as quoted in Eleanor McLaughlin's chapter "Christology in Dialogue with Feminist Ideology—Bodies and Boundaries," in *Christology in Dialogue*, ed. Robert F. Berkey and Sarah A. Edwards (Cleveland: Pilgrim, 1993), 313.

61. Johnson, *She Who Is*, 152.

62. Hampson, *Theology and Feminism*, 71.

63. See Delores Williams, "Black Women's Surrogacy and the Christian Notion of Redemption," in *After Patriarchy: Feminist Transformations of the World Religions*, ed. Paula M. Cooey, et al. (Maryknoll, N.Y.: Orbis, 1991), 1–14, and Rita Nakashima Brock, *Journeys by Heart: A Christology of Erotic Power* (New York: Crossroad, 1992).

64. Barbara Lundblad, "Re-Imagining Jesus: Reflections from the World Where Women Live," *Church and Society: Presbyterian Church, USA* 84, no. 5 (May/June 1994): 36.

65. Williams, "Black Women's Surrogacy," 12.

66. Johnson, *She Who Is*, 160.

67. Ibid.

68. See Christ, "Why Women Need the Goddess," 273–87.

69. It is also important to note that Lutenhaus-Lackey's sculpture of the crucified woman had neither a cross nor nail marks in the hands. See Doris Jean Dyke, *The Crucified Woman* (Toronto: United Church Publishing House, 1991), 15.

70. Ibid., 8.

71. Ibid., 26.

72. Ibid., 27.

73. Ibid., 49.

74. Ibid., 63.

75. See Flora Keshgegian's objections in *Redeeming Memories: A Theology of Healing and Transformation* (Nashville, Tenn.: Abingdon, 2000), 189.

76. *LW* 45:200.

77. *LW* 45:206.

78. Moltmann-Wendel, "A Feminist Theology of the Cross," 82.

79. See Sherry Jordon's extremely helpful study of Luther's treatment of women's ability to preach the Word of God in "Women as Proclaimers and Interpreters of the Word," *Currents in Theology and Mission* 24, no. 1 (February 1997): 33–43.

80. *LW* 45:100.

81. *LW* 44:131.

82. *LW* 21:316.

83. Johnson, *She Who Is,* 160–61.

84. *LW* 31:304.

85. Bernard Häring, *Free and Faithful in Christ: Moral Theology for Clergy and Laity,* vol. 2 (New York: Crossroad, 1984), 139, as quoted in Johnson, *She Who Is,* 161.

86. *LW* 31:342.

87. Jacquelyne Grant, *White Women's Christ and Black Women's Jesus: Feminist Christology and Womanist Response* (Atlanta, Ga.: Scholars, 1989), 144.

88. I propose that there be a variety of female bodies depicted as crucified, not simply one.

89. Brown and Parker, "For God So Loved the World?" 36.

90. Rita Nakashima Brock, "And a Little Child Will Lead Us," in Brown and Bohn, *Christianity, Patriarchy, and Abuse,* 52.

91. Parker, "The Unblessed Child," 211.

92. For Elizabeth Schüssler Fiorenza, "malestream discourse" is the discourse that has dominated tradition, and stands in opposition to feminist discourse. See *Jesus: Miriam's Child, Sophia's Prophet,* 3.

93. Brock, *Journeys by Heart,* 93.

94. Ibid., 94.

95. Ibid., 42.

96. Schüssler Fiorenza, *Jesus: Miriam's Child, Sophia's Prophet,* 123.

97. Johnson, *She Who Is,* 158.

98. Ibid., 159.

99. Ibid. Through her retrieval of the scriptural references to God as fully manifest in the form of *Sophia,* and through her insistence on the priority of women's experiences of God, Johnson renames God in the image of women, as *Sophia,* and ultimately as *She Who Is.*

100. Ibid., 168.

101. Dorothee Soelle, *Suffering,* trans. Everett Kalin (Philadelphia: Fortress Press, 1975), 42.

102. Ibid., 88.

103. Ibid., 139.

104. Ibid., 148.

105. Ibid., 164.

106. Schüssler Fiorenza, *Jesus: Miriam's Child, Sophia's Prophet,* 120.

107. Gerhard O. Forde, "The Work of Christ," in *Christian Dogmatics,* ed. Carl E. Braaten and Robert W. Jensen (Philadelphia: Fortress Press, 1984) and Mary Knutson, "Toward a Contemporary Theology of the Cross," Convocation Address (5 October 1995), Luther Seminary, St. Paul, Minnesota.

108. *LW* 31:350.

109. Michael Wallace, "The Atonement and Justice," *Theology* 7, 741 (May 1988): 182.

110. Ibid.

111. *LW* 1:288–89.

112. *LW* 37:219.

113. *LW* 2:143.

114. Johnson, *She Who Is*, 258.

115. McFague, *Metaphorical Theology*, 131.

116. Ibid., 159.

117. Forde, "The Work of Christ," 16.

118. Rowan Williams, *Christian Spirituality: A Theological History from the New Testament to Luther and St. John of the Cross* (Atlanta: John Knox, 1980), 154.

Chapter 5

1. Otto Pesch, "Free by Faith: Luther's Contribution to Theological Anthropology," in *Martin Luther and the Modern Mind: Freedom, Conscience, Toleration, Rights*, vol. 22, Toronto Studies in Theology, ed. Manfred Hoffman (Lewiston, N.Y.: Mellen, 1985), 41.

2. Ibid., 43.

3. Ann Pederson, "Conversations Toward an Ongoing Lutheran Reformation," *Currents in Theology and Mission* 24, no. 1 (February 1997): 10.

4. It is precisely the articulation of a theology of the cross in the North American context that Douglas John Hall does so powerfully. See in particular his trilogy, *Thinking the Faith: Christian Theology in a North American Context* (Minneapolis: Fortress Press, 1989), *Professing the Faith: Christian Theology in a North American Context* (Minneapolis, Fortress Press, 1993), and *Confessing the Faith: Christian Theology in a North American Context* (Minneapolis: Fortress Press, 1996).

5. Jaroslav J. Pelikan, *Luther the Expositor: Introduction to the Reformer's Exegetical Writings* (St. Louis: Concordia, 1959), 54–57.

6. Jewish feminist Amy-Jill Levine begins her essay on Sarah and Hagar by saying she intends to avoid what so often happens in pairings: that one element of the couple is rendered superior to the other. See her article "Settling at Beer-lahai-roi," in *Daughters of Abraham: Feminist Thought in Judaism, Christianity, and Islam*, ed. Yvonne Yazbeck Haddad and John L. Esposito (Gainesville: University of Florida Press, 2001), 12–34.

7. See, for example, Phyllis Trible, *Texts of Terror: Literary-Feminist Readings of Biblical Narratives* (Philadelphia: Fortress Press, 1984), and Delores S. Williams, *Sisters in the Wilderness: The Challenge of Womanist God-Talk* (Maryknoll, N.Y.: Orbis, 1993).

8. I am referring specifically to Amy-Jill Levine's fascinating treatment of Sarah and Hagar, "Settling at Beer-lahai-roi," as well as the more controversial perspectives of Savina J. Teubal's *Sarah the Priestess: The First Matriarch of Genesis* (Athens, Ohio: Swallow, 1984), and also her *Hagar the Egyptian: The Lost Tradition of the Matriarchs* (San Francisco: Harper & Row, 1990).

9. See Levine, "Settling at Beer-lahai-roi," 21–22.

10. See Williams, *Sisters in the Wilderness*, 17–18.

11. Teubal, *Hagar the Egyptian*, xxxvi.

12. Levine, "Settling at Beer-lahai-roi," 85.

13. Teubal, *Hagar the Egyptian*, 168.

14. See Mary Potter Engel, "Evil, Sin, and the Violation of the Vulnerable," in *Lift Every Voice: Constructing Christian Theology from the Underside*, ed. Susan Brooks Thistlethwaite and Mary Potter Engel (San Francisco: Harper & Row, 1990), 152–64.

15. Levine makes this argument, "Settling at Beer-lahai-roi," 18–19.

16. I do not want to suggest that the Sarah and Hagar story is the only biblical story of women that informs a feminist theology of the cross. Why I did not choose the rape of Tamar (a story that might challenge my current framework) has to do with my concern for the question of how we—the living victims and oppressors—still live and are called to live transformed lives.

17. Rowan Williams, *Resurrection: Interpreting the Easter Gospel* (Harrisburg, Pa.: Morehouse, 1994), 24. My argument in this section is indebted to Williams's interpretation of the resurrection apparitions of Christ.

18. Ibid., 25.

19. Ibid., 26.

20. Several Luther scholars make the point that Luther reinstated the resurrection to its proper place in theological reflection. See Gerhard O. Forde, *On Being a Theologian of the Cross: Reflections on Luther's Heidelberg Disputation, 1518* (Grand Rapids, Mich.: Eerdmans, 1997), 1, and Pelikan, *Luther the Expositor*, 179, as examples. Forde also characterizes Douglas John Hall's theology of the cross as limited to the crucifixion (Forde, *On Being a Theologian of the Cross*, 18). While I side with Forde and Pelikan on this, I also think that the reluctance to embrace the resurrection wholeheartedly is understandable. Sometimes Luther emphasizes the cross alone in a way that makes it all but impossible to glimpse the resurrection.

21. This is recorded from a white woman in Thistlethwaite's "Women in Crisis" course. See Susan B. Thistlethwaite, *Sex, Race, and God: Christian Feminism in Black and White* (New York: Crossroad, 1989), 93.

22. Williams, *Resurrection*, 15–16.

23. Kathleen Norris, *Amazing Grace: A Vocabulary of Faith* (New York: Riverhead, 1998), 167.

24. But "What about children?" one might ask. Rowan Williams suggests that while we do not want to diminish the sense in which children are victims, he also insists that the "innocence" of the child is due largely to the "unformed capacity for responsible choice." See Williams, *Resurrection*, 13. I also do not want to deny the horrible reality that countless persons die *as victims* at the hands of vicious perpetrators. The fact that they are victims in death, I want to argue, does not fully or adequately capture their entire lived identities.

25. Ibid., 41.

26. Ibid., 46.

27. Ibid.

28. Ibid., 46–47.

29. Flora Keshgegian, *Redeeming Memories: A Theology of Healing and Transformation* (Nashville, Tenn.: Abingdon, 2000), 179.

30. Williams, *Resurrection*, 52.

31. Gail R. O'Day, commentary on "John," in *The Women's Bible Commentary*, ed. Carol A. Newsom and Sharon H. Ringe (Louisville, Ky.: Westminster John Knox, 1992), 302.

32. See Walter Altmann, *Luther and Liberation: A Latin American Perspective*, trans. Mary M. Solberg (Minneapolis: Fortress Press, 1992), 1–11, and Dorothee Soelle with Shirley A. Cloyes, *To Work and To Love: A Theology of Creation* (Philadelphia: Fortress Press, 1984), 55–67.

33. Charles Lutz, "The Suffering of the World: Have Lutherans a Distinctive Service?" *Lutheran Forum* 12, no. 2 (1978): 7.

34. Ibid.

35. See Jacquelyn Grant's insightful treatment of servant language, "The Sin of Servanthood and the Deliverance of Discipleship," in *A Troubling in My Soul: Womanist Perspectives on Evil & Suffering*, Emilie M. Townes, ed. (Maryknoll, N. Y.: Orbis, 1993), 199-218.

36. Mary Hunt, *Fierce Tenderness: A Feminist Theology of Friendship* (New York: Crossroad, 1991), 1.

37. Both Hunt and McFague make this point (Hunt, *Fierce Tenderness*, 2, and Sallie McFague, *Metaphorical Theology: Models of God in Religious Language* [Philadelphia: Fortress Press, 1982], 156).

38. "A friend is someone you like and someone who likes you," McFague, *Metaphorical Theology*, 160.

39. Hunt, *Fierce Tenderness*, 92.

40. McFague, *Metaphorical Theology*, 164.

41. Altmann, *Luther and Liberation*, 66.

42. Sallie McFague, *Models of God: Theology for an Ecological, Nuclear Age* (Philadelphia: Fortress Press, 1987), 172.

43. Williams, *Resurrection*, 40.

44. Ibid., 68.

45 James Wood, "Two Kingdoms—in America?" *Currents in Theology and Mission* 14 (1989): 176.

46. Ibid., 162.

Index

Abraham saga, 84–89, 141–47

Adam, 81–83

alien work of God, 23–24, 51, 83, 133, 155

Althaus, Paul, 30

Anfechtung, 5–7, 10, 20, 23, 63–65, 69, 81–82, 107, 109–10, 132, 146, 153, 164

Antichrist, 42, 79

anti-Judaism, 89–91, 104, 124

Aristotle, 4–5, 8, 13–14, 41

atonement, xii–xiii, 25–26, 42–45, 57, 86–87, 107, 109, 110, 127–28, 131–37, 146

Augustine, 49

Aulen, Gustav, 26

baptism, 39, 41, 44, 79, 83, 158

Bertram, Robert, 75, 77, 90

Bible, books of:

   Acts, 149

   I Corinthians, 40

   Ephesians, 27

   Exodus, 24

   Galatians, 43

   Genesis, 80–89, 142–47

   Isaiah, 23, 121

   John, 136–38, 149, 153, 155, 156, 158

   Luke, 154

   Matthew, 137, 148

   I Peter, 40

   Philipians, 20

   Psalms, 6–7

   Revelation, 50

   Romans, 7, 9, 18, 76

Bora, Katharina von, 68

Boys, Mary, 101

Brecht, Martin, 80, 164, 168

Brock, Rita Nakashima, 118, 127–29

Brown, Joanne Carlson, 112–13, 127

Bussert, Joy M. K., 175

Chalcedon, Council of, 117

Charles V, 73–74

Christ, Carol, 98, 119

Christa, 119–21, 126

Christology, 99–100, 118, 123–24, 127–28, 130

coram Deo, 9, 10, 15–16, 18, 22, 24, 34–35, 38, 40, 45, 52, 59–61, 67, 81, 104, 106

coram hominibus, 18, 35, 45, 60–61

Crusades, ix

Daly, Mary, 99, 117, 174

Diet of Augsburg, 75–76, 78–79

Diet of Worms, 47–48, 75

disobedience, 85, 142–44

divine child abuse, 133

Dyke, Doris Jean, 119

Ebeling, Gerhard, 3, 7, 12, 15, 67, 81, 114

Eck, Johannes, 31–32

Edwards, Mark U., 67, 90–91

Elshtain, Jean Bethke, 176

Erasmus, 58–59, 61, 63–64, 67, 74

Eve, 81–83

faith, 11, 26, 34–35, 38–39, 44–48, 51, 81, 83, 100, 103, 106, 139–40, 142, 144, 146, 149, 155

feminist exegesis, 142–47

feminist theology, regarding:

   anti-Judaism, 104

   atonement, 127–35

   crucified woman, 119, 126, 149–53